HOW ON EARTH DID THAT HAPPEN?

HOW ON EARTH DID THAT HAPPEN?

~∾ When heaven and work collide ∾~

Roger Greene

This edition published in 2017 by Great Big Life Publishing
Empower Centre, 83-87 Kingston Road, Portsmouth, PO2 7DX, UK.

British Library Cataloguing in Publication Data. A catalogue record for this book is available from the British Library

ISBN-13: 978-0-9957925-0-0
ISBN-10: 099579250X
eBook ISBN: 978-0-9957925-1-7

CONTENTS

FOREWORD

∞

Picture a city on a hill at night, the skyline ablaze with lights that can be seen from miles around. Hear the sound of a voice, 'You are the light of the world. A city on a hill cannot be hidden ... let your light shine before men, that they may see your good deeds and praise your Father in heaven' (Matthew 5:14-16).

That picture and those words sum up what Roger has been seeking to live for many years in his business and work life. To pray and ask God for new clients and contracts, to ask God for wisdom and direction in a current piece of work, and to see God come through with answers and miraculous provision and intervention on a regular basis has become normal. God being at the centre of his career, business and work life to effect change in a business, an organisation or field of work has not only become normal, but essential.

Why essential? Because of a profound understanding and sense of call that God not only wants us to prosper in our work but that He wants us to be part of advancing His kingdom through transforming lives and the society in which we live through what we do.

Maybe that is not the story of most people. Maybe for many of us we have never really thought, let alone believed, that God wants to be at the heart of our work, for us to flourish and thrive in every aspect of our lives which includes our work life.

For a long time there has been a separation in many Christians' lives between their spiritual life and their career, business and work life. God never intended for there to be a sacred-secular divide in our thinking or in the church.

Perpetuating that has been the fact that many churches have focused on those with a call to vocational ministry within the church or to those called to overseas missions. This has led to the unintended consequence that many Christians have not been encouraged and empowered to see their work life as a call, a mission, something of value. They have simply seen it as a job to pay the bills or secondary to having a recognised ministry within the church. This has led to restriction and downsizing of the church's ability to be effective in sending people out to live the gospel message with full integrity in their business and work lives.

When God created man and put him in the Garden of Eden there was no sacred-secular divide. His purpose was for mankind to know Him, be fruitful, increase in number and fill the earth. As part of that God put him in the garden to work it and take care of it. We see right from the outset that work was part of life with God, not separate from God. Work was part of shaping Adam's day and purpose.

Therefore, every Christian is called into full-time ministry. Once we step over the line and begin to follow Jesus, everything we do is supposed to be done in His name, representing Him, with the goal of advancing the kingdom. Our workplaces are a key part of that and are one of the major ways in which God wants to effect change in people's lives and society.

Where did Jesus find some of His twelve disciples? In their workplace! Simon Peter, Andrew, James and John were all fishing, Matthew was collecting taxes.

When the apostle Paul first came to Europe, who was the first person to respond to the gospel? A business woman called Lydia who was a cloth trader.

As you read the stories and the biblical teaching and principles laid out by Roger you will be encouraged that God wants to be fully involved in your career, business and workplace, and that He wants to do powerful things in and through your life too.

God is turning the church inside out. He is seeking and sending out Jesus-following engineers, teachers, van drivers, nurses and entrepreneurs who are willing to ply their trade wherever they are needed to help the cause of the gospel. They understand that the front lines of evangelism and ministry are most often found in the marketplace, not within the four walls of our churches.

One of the measures of the stewardship of our lives will not necessarily be found in what happens in the church building on a Sunday but by what we do once we leave the building going into Monday.

Hearing the stories of what God has done in someone's everyday life and world can have the most life-impacting affect on us. Enjoy reading Roger's story and let faith be ignited for what God wants to do in and through you.

I believe this book is very timely for the church and a must-read for every Christian who ventures into the workplace.

Clive Urquhart
Senior Pastor
Kingdom Faith Church

How on Earth Did That Happen?

INTRODUCTION

∞

For many people their job is their very sense of identity and purpose in life. It marks their place in the world.

The world of work is also fundamental to the well-being of society. It is where monetary value is given to people's abilities, skills and roles. Jobs give people relative status and 'importance' in the eyes of society. Like it or not, you have to admit it's true.

Holding down a 'steady job' is seen as a sign of character and responsibility, the difference between success and failure in life. On the other hand, long-term unemployment can bring a sense of guilt and shame, with well-evidenced ill-effects on personal well-being and sense of value.

For most of us our jobs are the source of money to determine the kind of house and neighbourhood we live in, to feed and clothe the family, to determine what kind of car we can buy, if we can buy one at all. For the vast majority of Christians, it is the way the Lord chooses to provide for us.

So how come the church is so silent about the world of work?

How often, when you meet someone for the first time at church on a Sunday morning, do you hear them tell you about their 'secular' work as though it were some kind of incidental thing or shameful secret, a 'tent-making' job to feed the family while they pursue their ministry in the evenings and at weekends? Or until the church releases them into full-time ministry?

'Full-time ministry'. When did you ever hear that phrase used to describe the work of a painter and decorator, a bus driver, a social worker or a business executive? Where did you read the phrase in the Bible? It's like there's a parallel reality in the world of the church that excludes the very idea that being a heating engineer, a journalist or a sales assistant can be a calling from God and a genuinely spiritual vocation.

When was the last time someone in your church was prayed for before an important job interview or performance appraisal? Or invited to give their testimony to the church after winning a breakthrough sales pitch or employee of the month award?

Mainstream Christianity has separated the spiritual and secular worlds for far too long now. And unless that changes, what chance does the church have of bringing the transformational power of Christ into society if it ignores the very place most Christians encounter 'the world'?

Jesus taught the first disciples to pray

Our Father in heaven, hallowed be your name, your kingdom come, your will be done on earth as it is in heaven.
Matthew 6:9-10

On earth as it is in heaven!

Through the ages God has activated His people to respond prophetically to their times in practical ways. I believe He is now calling us – His church – to re-integrate the spiritual and the secular in our working lives, so as to transform society through the restoration of His kingdom values in the world of work.

How do I know?

I know because of what I have experienced over nearly three decades of my life in the world of work. I have had so many experiences that defy conventional business or human logic with such spooky regularity that I defy even the most cynical atheist to put them down to chance or luck.

They are the experiences that have led to the title of this book – *How On Earth Did That Happen?*

This is a book about the world of work and faith coming together. The marketplace comprises organisations full of individuals like you and me. It comprises organisations ranging from small businesses to large corporations, from local to national public service bodies, from local to international not-for-profit 'third sector' enterprises.

How often have you entered a high-street shop, factory or office building and felt welcome or unimportant, valued or in the way? How often have you felt a light or a heavy 'atmosphere' in a physical place but you can't pin it down to the behaviour of the individual people you meet?

Christians often talk about the 'life and spirit' of a church but we rarely hear anyone talk about the 'life and spirit' of a business or a public service organisation. I have often heard believers talk about the need for the church to adopt more learning from business, but I have rarely heard anyone talk about extending the principles of the Christian church into their workplaces and businesses.

We tend to think of organisations as disembodied and distant things we can't control or influence, full of people we call 'they' or 'the management', where bureaucracy is born but where we think no-one does 'real work'. This book is about showing how believers can truly and tangibly change the organisation around them and impact the spirit of the enterprise in which they work.

One of my underlying aims is to name and dismantle the false divide in the church between the sacred and the secular. I also want the church of Christ to change the way we think about organisations and understand they are also spiritual entities with spiritual life. Because of that you will hear a lot from me in this book about the welfare and financial standing of the organisations I have worked in. My 'how did that happen?' stories bear witness to God's interest in the health and welfare of the organisations in His creation and where His children work and where the vast majority receive His provision for their lives.

We need to get to biblical truth about our work and enterprise and their place in God's design purposes for our lives if we want to be agents of change in the society around us. It's not the only way, but it surely is at the centre of God's design purposes for His creation.

And that's what this book is about. It's a personal story I offer to encourage all believers to take their rightful place in the world of work and to be the difference the world so clearly needs right now!

One

THE MULTIPLICATION BUSINESS

∞

*And who knows but that you have come to royal position for such a
time as this?*

Esther 4:14

It all began in a conversation in 2008 between Paul and his brother
on the Victoria line train between Billingshurst and Horsham. Paul
was an information technology consultant and asked his brother, a
lawyer, what the legal industry needed from an IT system. The answer
was a system with twelve capabilities.

That conversation sparked Paul to develop a software solution,
which is basically an electronic 'bundle' of trial evidence for presentation
in court cases by lawyers and judges. As a result Paul and Bev
launched their company working from a corner of their dining-
room table in a West Sussex village.

In 2012 they thought converting two paper evidence bundles a
month into electronic bundles, for use in the courtroom, was a good
month. Four years later the conversion rate is two bundles per minute.
Talk about multiplication!

How on earth did that happen?

The answer is a collaborative partnership between Paul's gift for IT systems development and Bev's gift for intercessory prayer and prophecy. While Paul was busily developing the IT solution on the dining-room table, Bev had covered one of the dining-room walls with scripture and God's promises about business, constantly declaring them over the emerging company.

They experienced massive financial pressure during the development phase, but surrendered the business to the Lord and handed their financial situation over to Him. For example, they continued to tithe despite their debt, and when Bev had a dream that there was something wrong with part of the IT system architecture, Paul discovered that he was using a copied piece of inexpensive software for which he hadn't paid a licence fee. So despite the mounting debts he bought a licence. They put God's standards above their financial plight.

They stood on the Word of God as He spoke to them from Romans 8:31:

If God is for us, who can be against us?

Then in 2013 Paul was called to a brainstorm meeting with the Ministry of Justice (MoJ), along with thirty other companies. The MoJ wanted to tap the brains of the industry to work out a way to get rid of the overwhelming volumes of paper that plagued the system and make the courts' systems paperless. As Paul heard them describe the ambition he immediately realised he already had the answer.

To cut a long story short, the MoJ began a major engagement process, inviting over forty companies to suggest plans to develop and deliver the solution. In the final procurement phase it came down to a shortlist of two: Paul and Bev's company, working out of a dining room in a village in West Sussex, and an international IT systems provider with 68,000 staff globally.

When Bev was praying about the selection interview she saw angels enter the room when Paul went in, and then saw them leave when the competitors went in. Paul went into the interview knowing he had heavenly company. And then there was what seemed like an interminable wait of months to hear the result (anyone who has experienced a Government procurement process will nod in recognition!). So Paul, a man who confesses to really enjoying his food, committed to fasting until they got the contract. His fast lasted four hours!

The contract was awarded to them in March 2015 and went live in March 2016. As a result the Criminal Courts of England and Wales are now paperless, saving 2,000 trees a month, and the system has 18,000 users with secure electronic access to criminal evidence for judges, prosecution and defence lawyers, and administrative staff. Every month it sends 2.3 million pages of electronic evidence securely for 9,000 court cases.

God loves justice as well as believers in business. The impact on the efficiency of the Criminal Justice System in England and Wales has been massive. For those of you who like facts and figures to back up the claim, here are a few:

- The number of hearings required to resolve a guilty plea in the Crown Courts has reduced by 50 per cent.
- Guilty pleas are being submitted much earlier because all the evidence is available to all key parties at the click of a mouse – no more lost or missing bits of paper evidence.
- There has been a significant upward trend in early guilty pleas, giving swifter results for victims, witnesses and defendants.

So how did that happen?

Paul and Bev committed their business completely to God. They sought the guidance of the Holy Spirit for their practical steps and held faithfully to the prophetic words the Lord had given them. They held their accountability to God above their material circumstances even in times of extreme financial pressure.

And that's how God multiplied their business from two bundles a month to two bundles a minute!

And by the way, they now operate out of offices in Victoria. They didn't know the name of the office suite until they occupied it. It was already called Buckingham Palace. 'And who knows but that you have come to royal position for such a time as this?'

Paul and Bev's story is one of faith, perseverance and intercessory prayer wrapped around business skills, dreams and vision. It is one of many people you will find in this book. Like Richard, for example.

My friend Richard is one of the most unassuming men of God you will ever meet. He is shy and shuns away from the limelight. However, he has an extraordinary gift from God for steel fabrication (or welding, for the uninitiated) – though I tend to think of his work as sculpture more than functional steel fabrication.

He works for a well-known company on the south coast and has gained a reputation over the years for doing the kind and quality of work no-one else can do. It's the sort of stuff no-one can design, draw or plan because it's so technically difficult. So whenever a client comes to the company with an 'impossible dream', Richard's managing director goes to him and leaves it with him. Richard not only prays, but prays in full faith, confidence and expectation that the Holy Spirit will give him the answer in dreams and visions during his sleep. And that's exactly how it works. The Lord never fails to come up with the solution in Richard's dreams. He wakes up with the answers to the design issues, and never fails to deliver on the client assignment. His work features in landmark places in London in particular – the Olympic stadium, Wembley Stadium, London Bridge, Paddington Basin and Canary Wharf to name but a few of the prestige sites he has worked on.

These are just a couple of my friends where heaven and work collide to produce extraordinary results through ordinary people. Just like you and me.

Two

THERE BE DRAGONS!

∞

You will never get back the time you spend reading this book, so it's only polite if I say a little bit more about myself. That way you can have a reality check before you embark on the journey with me. I reckon you're entitled to know a bit about me if you are going to invest a few hours of your life in my story. Fair enough?

I grew up as a Roman Catholic kid in Liverpool in the 1950s and 60s, and I just wanted to play football. Usually in the street. I didn't know trees could grow on streets until I moved house at the age of 12. I never wanted to be an altar-boy.

Then I passed the selection thing they called the 11 Plus to go to a Grammar school that played rugby. I was gutted there was no football, but I soon fell in love with rugby, cricket and athletics. I had no career vision or ambitions at all, and the sports I played were mainly amateur those days so there was no prospect of a career there, even if I had been good enough.

I more or less drifted into university because it felt like the right thing to do (and no tuition fees to consider!). No pressure from my parents, both of whom had left school at 14 or 15 in the 1930s and suffered the horrors of the Second World War in the early years of their marriage, including three years for my dad as a prisoner of war in Italian and

German concentration camps. They knew the importance of education, but also the importance of letting their children find their own way.

I studied Spanish and Portuguese for my university degree, mainly because I found learning foreign languages relatively easy. Maths and Chemistry were too much like hard work. Did I have a vision for my life? At the age of 21 I wouldn't have understood the question if you had asked me.

I guess I have then had an unusual career over the subsequent forty years.

Despite getting married at 25 I managed to drag my education out until I was 27, researching for a PhD that added very little to the sum of human endeavour or knowledge. But it was great fun (at the taxpayers' expense again – sorry, but thank you!) and gave me the chance to teach English abroad for a couple of years while I decided what I wanted to research before I got a 'proper' job with a pension scheme – after all I was married now and would soon have family responsibilities. Such were my ambitions at that pretty carefree stage of life.

So I tinkered with academia for a while, but couldn't find a permanent job. As a result, I went into the UK National Health Service as a graduate management trainee in 1980, basically because they were the first people to offer me a job. Though in fairness (I'm speaking to myself now) I did want to do something working in public service for the public good. I suppose that was a vision of sorts starting to take shape.

I spent over twenty years in the NHS, the last twelve of which were as a Chief Executive of a couple of NHS Trusts, in an environment where the average annual 'churn rate' for CEOs is about a third every year. Hard to believe, but the role had (and still has) a higher turnover than Premier League football managers. But more of that later.

In 2005 I decided to move out of the public sector and into the world of commercial consultancy. This period included a three-year stint for two days a week as a CEO in a Christian charity as part of my consulting portfolio.

And in 2008 I was invited to buy in and become a co-owner and director of a commercial consultancy called Tricordant. We describe ourselves as a Commercial Christian Fellowship. More about that later.

So I have worked in public service, the third sector and the commercial sector in the UK. Indeed, I have held leadership positions in each of those sectors. While I know I'm not unique in that, it is quite a rare and privileged mix of experience.

I was brought up as a Roman Catholic, but fell away from faith during my teenage years into my thirties, and really only discovered a personal relationship with God in my mid-thirties. Strangely enough I cannot tell you when I was born again, because I didn't have a conversion experience, just a gradual sense of drawing closer to God. But again, more of that later.

But you want to know what all this 'There be Dragons' stuff in the chapter title is about, so let's move on to that.

My dragons

Now I'm older (and allegedly wiser) it's easy to see how my belief system built up in my childhood, teens and early twenties to the point where my adult spiritual life was surrounded by imaginary dragons, hemming me in and keeping me in line.

There was a jazz song playing regularly on the radio in the 1950s and one verse stuck in my head. You know how things you hear in your formative years stick with you as 'truths' basically because you've been exposed to them in an unquestioning way. It kept repeating the verse '*money is the root of all evil*'.

Now some songs stick in your head but don't affect the way you look at life. I grew up in Liverpool in the 1960s immersed in the 'pop' revolution, but somehow Eleanor Rigby 'wearing the face that she keeps in a jar by the door', while definitely memorable, didn't persuade me that people kept a spare face in the jar by the door (I really was that literal in my interpretations of songs back then!). And yet a jazz singer somehow got it into my head that money was the root of all evil. Therefore, as a young Roman Catholic boy I believed that God frowned on money. To compound it all, this evil stuff called money even had a name, mammon, like a competing divinity trying to knock God off His throne.

I went through my adolescent years in a Christian Brothers school, taught by other-worldly men dressed in cassocks and sandals who had given up all pretext of material comfort or wealth creation. I was taught that it is harder for a rich man to enter the kingdom of God than for a camel to get through the eye of a needle. Naturally that got into my belief system too.

Next came the university days when everyone who believed in Jesus Christ also believed He was really the first communist. Christians were people admirable for giving up any pursuit of material gain, had wild hair, sang 'Kumbaya', strummed guitars and wore sandals like the Christian Brothers of my school days. They rode bicycles and wore cycle-clips all day. Never quite all there. Not really in touch with reality. No rugby players among them. They might end up with a decent academic career playing with the unreal and esoteric. But entrepreneurs, managers and public leaders climbing the greasy pole of recognition and career success? Not really.

Now I know things are different today. Christian Unions in universities are way more attuned to contemporary life and the whole appeal of the church is so much more youth-oriented and 'cool'. Bands like Delirious and Switchfoot have changed the face of mainstream Christian music, while churches like Hillsong and Bethel have taken worship to a whole new level for new generations of believers. But still it's rare for CUs or the church to encourage the youth and young adults of today into any vocation other than mission or ministry.

Hopefully you're getting the picture. Your upbringing was probably very different to mine, and maybe you didn't go through your education with any kind of religious or faith background. It doesn't matter. Whether you believed in God or not, whether you believed in Jesus as the Son of God or not is immaterial. My bet is that you grew up thinking that money, material prosperity, powerful jobs and the like were incompatible or, at best, uncomfortable companions for religious faith, and that God frowns upon wealth and wealth creation. Maybe you still do. And Jesus, because you believed Him to be the precursor to socialism and communism, was bound to hate capitalism. So it's pretty obvious that Christianity is going to be anti-capitalist and anti-wealth creation. Isn't it? And anyway religion is really the source of all trouble and war in the world, so what could a book like the Bible possibly tell us about business and the workplace?

So before I could remotely think that God was interested in my working career and my prosperity, I had to slay a few of the dragons that besieged my youthful (and not so youthful) understanding. Like the following:

Dragon 1: Faith is for Sundays not workdays

I don't know about you, but I had always found it quite natural to compartmentalise life into different boxes: this box for family, that one for social life, another for recreation, a different one for work, and yet another box (quite a little one actually) for religion and church. And apart from school-days, when there had been daily assemblies with mandatory psalms or hymns, and voluntary Friday services, the 'church' box only ever got opened on a Sunday, and then only for a relatively brief period in the morning, or a fortnightly Saturday evening for confession when everything that happened when the church box was closed got forgiven. The availability of that Saturday evening slot in the confessional, followed by some Hail Marys and Our Fathers as penance (according to the seriousness of the sins I confessed) meant the slate got wiped clean regularly enough for me not to worry what happened in the other boxes on a day-to-day basis. So I grew up thinking religion was something parallel to the rest of my life. It helped me to be a 'good person', but otherwise I assumed the study of the Bible was really only for people in church ministry or for religious zealots.

When I progressed to the work phase of my life, the religion/church box only got opened something like once a fortnight because the rest of the time I thought it was important for me to achieve the right 'work-life balance' between family, recreation and work. So anything remotely spiritual in my life got squeezed out. A bit like with money, my church upbringing taught me nothing about work and its purpose. And why should it? After all, isn't it obvious that the purpose of work is to provide for our families and fulfil our potential as people?

While I knew that it wasn't right to operate double standards between work and the rest of my life, it never even occurred to me that the Bible could have anything remotely relevant to say about what I did at work. Admit it, that's what you thought as well, isn't it? It never occurred to me that the Bible might even have an opinion on work. But it does.

This dragon was for me a sleeping dragon that lay across my path and obstructed me rather than one who actively drove me down a particular road of belief (or disbelief) with its fiery breath.

What does the Bible say about work?

In Genesis 2, at the very beginning of the story of Creation, just after God has created Adam, it says:

> The LORD God took the man and put him in the Garden of Eden to work it and take care of it.
>
> **Genesis 2:15**

Here the Bible establishes work as a primary task for man. God's purpose was for man not just to live in and enjoy the fruits of the Garden of Eden, but to *work* it. And this was *before* the Fall, not after. According to the Bible, therefore, man's need to work was not the result of the original sin of eating the forbidden fruit, but is at the very core of man's purpose.

Elsewhere the Bible is very clear about the spiritual principles concerning the world of work.

In Proverbs, we read:

One who is slack in his work is brother to one who destroys.

Proverbs 18:9

Just working isn't enough. Working slackly is tantamount to being a destroyer. Whoops!

And what if we can't find a job? Surely then the State can look after us, because we've paid our taxes and national insurance contributions. Read on:

If a man will not work, he shall not eat.

2 Thessalonians 3:10

Not only must we work:

Whatever you do, work at it with all your heart, as working for the Lord, not for men.

Colossians 3:23

Not only does the Bible say God created man to work, it also says a man must work if he wants to eat. What's more he must work diligently.

Please get off my back if you're thinking that's a bit harsh on those unable to work for reasons of ill-health or disability. I'm not judging. I'm simply repeating what the Bible says about work. It has plenty of other more charitable things to say about love for one another, compassion for those who suffer disadvantage, feeding the hungry and clothing the poor, but that's a separate subject I'm not going to cover here.

Sleepy Dragon 1 evaporated in a puff of smoke when I realised the relevance of biblical teaching to my work and career. According to the Bible I was actually created to work, and then not just to work for the sake of it. I was created to work 'as working for the Lord'.

In other words there is no division in the teaching of the Bible between our work lives and our spiritual lives. They are one and the same.

Dragon 2: Money is the root of all evil

As Bible-believing Christians will know, the jazz singer of my childhood had got it wrong. But she sang me into believing money was evil. A necessary evil, but evil just the same. It took me thirty years to discover the Bible actually says something rather different. It says:

For the love of money is a root of all kinds of evil.
1 Timothy 6:10

The Bible does not say that money is evil. My jazz singer sang what she thought it said, or maybe what her parents told her it said. Or maybe what her preacher told her it said. But it doesn't say it. It says something close but subtly different. It says that *loving* money is what's wrong. Not *having* it. *Loving* it. And it's not *the* root. It's *a* root. One of several, not the only one.

Money tends to be a dirty subject in churches. It's rarely ever preached about. Even less is it taught about. I was never taught about money in my traditional church upbringing, or at school come to think of it. And unless you were brought up knowing directly what the Bible says, rather than through a third party, your experience was probably not that different to mine. The plate would go around for the collection and everyone was embarrassed into slipping some loose change in to make the gesture. So who taught me to think it was evil? My jazz singer did. And the silence of my church on the subject meant I wasn't disabused of my misunderstanding. Because my jazz singer was the only one who bothered to teach me anything about the moral or spiritual dimension of money at all at that stage of my life. So I grew up thinking it was a necessary evil, but evil nonetheless.

You will see from my stories later on that God really cares about our financial welfare, to the extent that He has positively and miraculously intervened on numerous occasions to sort them out for me both corporately and personally.

It wasn't until I started to read the Bible for myself that I discovered what I *believed* the Bible said about money was wrong. Knowing it wasn't evil left me a bit puzzled, however, because I'd heard that rich men could not enter the kingdom of heaven. This takes me on to Dragon 3.

Dragon 3: Rich men, camels and needles' eyes

We have all heard this one, haven't we? This is the bit of the Bible where Jesus tells the rich young man to sell all his possessions and give the proceeds to the poor, so he can have treasure in heaven. Jesus then goes on to say:

> *'How hard it is for the rich to enter the kingdom of God!' The disciples were amazed at his words. But Jesus said again, 'Children, how hard it is to enter the kingdom of God! It is easier for a camel to go through the eye of a needle than for a rich man to enter the kingdom of God.' The disciples were even more amazed, and said to each other, 'Who then can be saved?' Jesus looked at them and said, 'With man this is impossible, but not with God; all things are possible with God.'*
>
> **Mark 10:23-27**

My dragon had been my *partial* knowledge of the scripture. I was only familiar with the bit that seemed to make it impossible for a rich man to enter heaven. Other bits of the Bible say clearly that one cannot serve both God and money (Matthew 6:24 and Luke 16:13), so it all tied up in my mind to mean that wealth was frowned upon by God.

What I didn't know was that Jesus, as He so often did, was using a culturally-sensitive illustration to make His point. In Jerusalem there was a narrow gate in the city walls called the eye of a needle. A camel could not get through standing up and carrying a load. It could if it was unencumbered and went through on its knees. The disciples, as was occasionally the case, were a bit slow to pick up the subtlety. But the big point is more what Jesus said to conclude the discussion and which seldom gets quoted:

'With man this is impossible, but not with God; all things are possible with God.'

All things are possible with God. That includes the salvation of the rich man. What Jesus meant was that no-one can save themselves; only God can give the gift of salvation.

What about not being able to serve both God and money? That's exactly what the Bible does say. In fact it says it twice, once in Matthew's Gospel and again in Luke's Gospel. The answer is the same as for Dragon 2 really. It's not having money that offends God. It's *serving* money that displeases Him.

Slaying this dragon was a bit more difficult than Dragon 2 because this time the Bible actually says what I thought it said. The trick here is that the complete scripture says much more than the verse people are most familiar with. Okay, the allusion to the eye of the needle, the camel and the Jerusalem gate is a lot more obscure and you wouldn't get that from reading the scripture. But even if you didn't know that, you would still get the meaning that nothing is impossible for God, and that includes the salvation of a rich man.

Dragon 4: Proper Christians wear sandals and drive clapped-out cars

Dragon 3 made me believe that rich people who went to church were really hypocrites. I thought they went to church to alleviate their consciences. The real Christians, or so I thought, were the ones who looked as though they didn't have two pound coins to rub together because they always gave the spare one away to the church re-roofing fund. They lived in contented poverty and usually did socially responsible jobs with a touch of altruism about them like teaching, nursing or social work. I don't mean to demean those professions in the least, but you get my point about the stereotyping of Christians. Teacher – yes. Entrepreneur – no. Nurse – yes. Car dealer – no. And of course this clever little dragon (I'm talking about number 4 now – keep up!) got me thinking you could only be a proper Christian if you drove a modest kind of car. Ford Escort – yes. BMW – no. Vauxhall Astra – yes. Mercedes Benz – no. And so it went on. The observant amongst you will of course realise that Dragon 4 is really the off-spring of Dragons 2 and 3. Can you see how easily these false beliefs and prejudices build up?

Dragon 4 got well and truly blitzed for me by a pastor at my church in the mid-1990s, who declared one day when he was preaching that he and his wife had set their hearts on having a new people carrier, a 7-seater Ford Galaxy. And by the way, they weren't going to settle for anything less than top of the range. After all, he argued, why should they settle for second best when God's will is for us to prosper. He preached from Jeremiah 29:11, where God says to His people;

> *'For I know the plans I have for you,' declares the LORD, 'plans to prosper you and not to harm you, plans to give you hope and a future.'*

He showed us a whole group of Old Testament scriptures full of references to how God wants His people to prosper materially as well as spiritually. Here are a few examples:

> *You may say to yourself, 'My power and the strength of my hands have produced this wealth for me.' But remember the LORD your God, for it is he who gives you the ability to produce wealth, and so confirms his covenant, which he swore to your forefathers, as it is today.*
> **Deuteronomy 8:17-18**

> *The blessing of the LORD brings wealth, and he adds no trouble to it.*
> **Proverbs 10:22**

> *Humility and fear of the LORD bring wealth and honour and life.*
> **Proverbs 22:4**

Wow! Dragon 4 had as much chance of surviving as a snowman

sculpted with a blowtorch. I realised that the Bible doesn't frown on prosperity – it says that God gives it. It's how we respond that counts.

Honour the LORD *with your wealth, with the firstfruits of all your crops.*

Proverbs 3:9

It's not what we have but how we use it. We are to honour God with the wealth He gives us. And how, I can hear you say, do we do that? And what's all this stuff about 'firstfruits'. Stick with me. That comes later.

So what?

I don't know whether my dragons are your dragons. Maybe they are. Or maybe you have different dragons. Maybe you have never even asked yourself what your dragons are. In which case you should.

But just in case you recognised some of mine and you nodded as you read, here's what I have learned through using the Bible to slay my dragons:

- The Creation story in Genesis tells us that work is at the heart of God's purpose for mankind. We were designed to work.

- Christianity and the Bible do not hold money as intrinsically evil as long as it doesn't become an idol and take the place of God in our lives.

- The Bible has no problem with wealth and prosperity. Actually it shows a God who wants His people to prosper, and who were not created for poverty. Being rich doesn't mean automatic condemnation to eternal hell-fire.

- The Bible does not frown on material prosperity as sinful of its own accord. Indeed, it can be God's blessing. The distinction is that we cannot *serve* God and money. God can, however, bless us with money if we serve Him.

We will return to these and related themes throughout the book as we construct our vision of the kind of worker God would desire us to be 'on earth as it is in heaven'.

Three

AVODAH

Hurricane Katrina literally wiped out the Hancock Bank 17-storey HQ building in downtown Gulfport, Mississippi. They lost everything there: corporate computer operations, their technology hub, cheque-processing, loan-servicing and all other critical elements of their banking operation across four states. Only because of well-rehearsed emergency planning were they able to reopen technical operations three days later, ahead of other banks in the area, by transferring their HQ systems to their operations in Chicago.

However, it was what they decided to do before the Chicago facilities were online that truly shows the spirit of the organisation. The senior team noted that there was no mention of the word 'profit' in the bank's 1899 Charter. Their mandate was to serve people and take care of communities. Their purpose was to keep people's money safe and make money available. Their chairman had drilled into their heads that banking is impossible without assuming that at least 99 per cent of people are honest. They would stay true to their 'identity' and serve their community by providing money. They decided to allow people, whether they were Hancock Bank customers or not, to draw up to $200 cash if they could simply write out their name, address and Social Security number on a scrap of paper.

So on the Tuesday after the storm, ten branches opened without electricity or computers and gave money out to people, whoever they were, on the back of simple IOUs. Because of this Hancock Bank put $42 million in cash into the community in the week after the storm, $3.5 million of which went out to people who could not later be linked to any Hancock account or working phone.

And what happened? Did they lose all that money? All but $200,000 eventually came back to the bank as people recovered from the disaster and remembered Hancock Bank's trust in them and their IOU. And in the months afterwards overall deposits grew by $1.5 billion as new people chose Hancock Bank to be guardians of their money for the future. The spirit of the organisation, vested in the bank's leadership, courageously served the population and grew the business as a result!

It ain't what you do, it's the way that you do it

Or is it?

Here we go again. Another verse from another song. What do we reckon to this one for our belief system?

We already established from Genesis 2:15 that, even in our pre-Fall state, God designed us to work.

Avodah

Intriguingly the Hebrew word used for work in Genesis 2:15 is *avodah*. And *avodah* is held by some to mean three things in the Bible: work, worship, and service.[1] God gave us work as both acts of worship and of service. Is that how you see your job?

This raises the question whether all work is good work and pleasing to God. We'll come back to that shortly.

Avodah work is more than activity to earn a living. It has a deeper purpose. In my company Tricordant we describe meaningful and satisfying work as 'whole work'. But more about that in chapter eight.

---

1   I am aware some Bible scholars agree *avodah* means work and service to the Lord, but do not agree it means worship. I do not propose to discuss that polemic here.

If you are a heating engineer, is your purpose to install and fix heating systems? Or does it have a higher purpose to ensure people can live in safe, comfortable and affordably heated homes?

If you are a salesperson, is your purpose to sell product and boost your commission? Or is it to serve your customer and ensure they buy the best product or service for their needs? Even if that means less sales commission for you or no sale at all?

Think about it for a moment. What is the purpose of your job? Can you think of its higher purpose? Can you think of a way in which it serves God and is an expression of worship? Can you think of how it serves humanity or benefits society?

The extent to which an individual's work is meaningful to them is deeply personal. It depends heavily on their connection with the purpose of the organisation in which they work. People will volunteer their time and skills for no pay at all in values-driven charities, and yet those same people can hold down well-paid jobs in organisations whose basic purpose they don't understand and where they only stay to serve their career ambition or feed their families.

Commercial enterprises often have more difficulty in engaging their people in their purpose, which may seem to be more about making money and profit, in a competitive consumer market than it is about 'doing good'. Classically we think about a doctor or nurse doing more 'social good' and being able to serve God more than an entrepreneur. And yet the entrepreneur may be creating hundreds or thousands of jobs, giving many people meaningful work, enabling them to fulfil their God-given talents, and generating the very taxes that pay for the doctor or the nurse. Equally the security or cleaning company in your hospital, office block or warehouse may not be doing the same work as you, but the quality of their work determines whether the conditions for you to work in, and where patients or customers are taken care of, are pleasant, clean, safe and hygienic. The work they do is fully capable of serving God if their hearts are set on Him.

We see many large organisations turn their energies to 'corporate social responsibility' projects, to engage their people in work with an altruistic angle. How many of us have flown with the airlines that show you the video of the Third World country where your spare foreign currency can help supply clean water to eradicate disease? Even better, where the airline sends its crews of volunteers to go and work to help the local people, engaging their staff personally in the vision and 'good works'. Businesses like the Body Shop, where the founder's vision articulated passionately the case for preservation of the planet's natural resources and the institution of humane product-testing regimes, stimulated a whole corporate responsibility movement but also made good profits and business sense in the process. This illustrates the corporate search to connect with people's deep purpose and spirituality in its widest sense, but without necessarily placing God at the centre.

The point is that if an enterprise is to flourish and grow it needs to know what it's there for. It needs to know its purpose. And it needs its people to know its purpose. Do you know why your employer or your business exists?

And this raises the next question. Does having a clear purpose make work good work that is potentially pleasing to God?

Self-evidently not all purpose is good purpose. How do we know? Sometimes we are only able to distinguish with the perspective of history. To take an extreme example, Hitler's vision and mission must have seemed good to his followers as he preached Aryan supremacy. It must have appealed to something deep within them to cause them not only to persecute their enemies, but to lay their own lives on the line in so doing. Of course many would have done so through fear or selfish ambition, but many must also have believed (however misguidedly) in the truth of the enterprise. They must have done so to value human life so cheaply. But to the victims of his mission and in the perspective of history, Hitler's vision was and remains the incarnation of evil.

But before we get carried away by moral outrage at such enterprises, let's not forget that contemporary Western governments sought first appeasement rather than confronting the atrocities Hitler and his followers committed in pursuit of their goals. Hitler stands condemned by history and the perspective of time. But at the time the appeasers nearly held sway among Western governments. Things are never quite as black and white at the time as they appear through the retrospectoscope of history.

Integrity of the enterprise

But you will rightly say that we need to know about the ethical and moral quality of the places we work *now* and can't wait for history's verdict. So how can we tell?

Jesus' words in Luke 6:43-44 give the biblical answer:

No good tree bears bad fruit, nor does a bad tree bear good fruit. Each tree is recognised by its own fruit.

The apostle James gives a similar message:

Out of the same mouth come praise and cursing. My brothers, this should not be. Can both fresh water and salt water flow from the same spring? My brothers, can a fig-tree bear olives, or a grapevine bear figs? Neither can a salt spring produce fresh water.

James 3:10-12

In other words, what determines the quality of an enterprise is the outcome of the service or product.

As with vision, not all enterprise is good enterprise. Some is positively immoral and unethical. Some is positively moral and ethical. Does it matter to God? And should it matter to you?

Do you remember Dragon 3 in chapter two? The one that stereotyped Christians as wearing sandals and driving clapped-out cars? The one that had me believe you could not be a Christian and an entrepreneur or a car dealer? Dragon 3 persuaded me to make value judgements based on my (often mistaken) thoughts or stereotypes about the ethics and integrity of people who do a particular type of work.

I believe the vast majority of enterprises and professions can have a fundamentally good purpose from an ethical and moral standpoint. Let's look at some examples:

- professional athlete
- shopkeeper
- second-hand car dealer
- magazine publisher
- dancer

Which of the five is intrinsically ethical or unethical?

Is a professional athlete more or less ethical because of the sport they play? The sport of track and field athletics is amongst the most ancient and considered amongst the most noble. Man against man, woman against woman. *Citius, altius, fortius.* Speed and endurance tested to their limits to find the fastest and strongest athletes in the world, illuminated by the noble flame of the Olympic ideal. *Chariots of Fire* and all that.

Then came anabolic steroids. Ben Jonson and the 1987 World Championships blew apart the innocence of athletics as a noble sport dependant solely on an athlete's natural talent. The twenty-first-century version of the sport is riven with suspicion every time an athlete runs that bit faster or jumps that bit further than their peers, especially if their personal level of improvement is out of the ordinary. Is the sport intrinsically any more or less ethical or noble than when Jesse Owen sprinted and jumped to victory in front of Hitler in Berlin in 1936? No. What has changed is man's ability to secure advantage, even if unethically gained, through the development of performance-enhancing drugs. The sport is no less noble. It's some of the players who are less noble.

Is a sport more or less ethical because of the money it pays its star performers? Basketball, golf and motor sports pay their stars millions of pounds a year to entertain their fans, and millions more in endorsements. Was the basketball played by Michael Jordan more or less ethical than a backyard game played for fun? Is golf as played by Rory McIlroy more or less ethical than a 'gaffers' Wednesday-morning four-ball at the local club? In both cases the answer is negative, unless we ask a different question about whether the businesses that run the sports played by these icons commercially exploit both their fans and the producers of their merchandise. And that's where the issue enters about the 'spirit of the business', illustrating how sport, for example, can be exploited by unethical brands and businesses who source their merchandise from sweat shops and child labour. Complicated, isn't it?

Is a shopkeeper more or less ethical because they sell electrical goods rather than food? Is a second-hand car dealer more or less ethical than a dealer in new cars? Is a magazine publisher more or less ethical than a book publisher? And so on. The answer, of course, is they can all be ethical or unethical, dependant on their focus and approach.

Take the magazine publisher. Is the publisher of pornographic magazines more or less ethical than the publisher of *Golf Monthly*? As a pastime golf is probably neither intrinsically ethical nor unethical, though of course golf nuts would have you believe it teaches ethical behaviour, and maybe it does as long as it is played honourably. It can of course be played ethically or unethically, but in itself the game of golf is probably ethically neutral. Can pornography ever be ethical? So-called soft porn is often thought to be harmless and just a bit of fun. But can it ever be ethical if it feeds sexual exploitation, infidelity and immorality? Not by biblical standards.

What about selling cars? An extreme viewpoint might say all car sales are unethical because of the impact of the car on the environment. Yet the car serves to transport families to work, to school, on holiday and to many places of benefit they could not otherwise go. What is it that makes us believe being a second-hand car dealer is less respectable (proxy for ethical) than a dealer in new cars? After all many families needing personal transport cannot afford a new car. What they need is reliable and affordable transport. Dismiss your thoughts of Arthur Daley for a moment and admit it is nonsense to believe a dealer in good quality, good value second-hand cars is any less ethical in what they do than the new-car dealer. What makes all the difference is how they do what they do, and whether they are there simply to chase the sale or serve the client.

The dancer? Is ballet more ethical than lap-dancing? What about the dancer who does both? The ballet will be ethical if the subject-matter is ethical. Lap-dancing, however, can never claim to be ethical and the dancer would probably laugh at the mere suggestion that their work should be judged within a moral/ethical biblical framework.

We could go on, but by now I hope you get the picture. The integrity of an enterprise depends upon how they do what they do. Some enterprises clearly lack integrity ethically and morally regardless of how they are performed. An enterprise involved in pornography, prostitution or drug-dealing can never claim ethical integrity, and would probably never even want to. Some drug dealers take pride in the purity and quality of their products. But how can enterprises that purposely develop and exploit addiction to illegal substances ever claim an ethical basis?

Conversely there are enterprises that would appear intrinsically good. Medicine is a classic example. In the biblical context Jesus came to heal the sick and give sight to the blind. That is precisely what doctors aim to do. But are all doctors ethical doctors? The overwhelming majority certainly conduct themselves within a strict ethical framework, and medicine as a profession has been amongst the first to embrace an explicit ethical code through the Hippocratic Oath. Ethics committees are woven into the structural fabric of healthcare in the UK. And yet Harold Shipman has passed into criminal history as Britain's biggest mass murderer. Florence Nightingale set the global iconic standard for nursing, but Beverley Allitt was a children's nurse and was convicted as a serial killer in 1993.

But neither Shipman nor Allitt make all doctors and nurses potential murderers-in-waiting either. They were both serial killers who exploited the vulnerability and trust of their patients at their times of greatest need.

This is complicated stuff, isn't it? So can we simplify it? Is there a practical framework to guide Christians in making these ethical and moral distinctions about the integrity of an enterprise?

The single passage of biblical scripture that best enables judgements to be made about the quality of the 'fruit' of an enterprise is Paul's letter to the Galatians:

> *The acts of the sinful nature are obvious: sexual immorality, impurity and debauchery; idolatry and witchcraft; hatred, discord, jealousy, fits of rage, selfish ambition, dissensions, factions and envy; drunkenness, orgies, and the like. I warn you, as I did before, that those who live like this will not inherit the kingdom of God. But the fruit of the Spirit is love, joy, peace, patience, kindness, goodness, faithfulness, gentleness and self-control.*
>
> **Galatians 5:19-23**

For the vast majority of enterprises, it is *both* what you do *and* the way that you do it. And you can judge the integrity with which the job is being done by whether the product creates a set of reactions that belong in the first or the second group that Paul describes. Does the enterprise engender 'the acts of the sinful nature' or 'the fruit of the Spirit'? Remember Dragon 1. Making money is not intrinsically good or bad. It's the love of money that is the root of all kinds of evil.

'Those who live like this will not inherit the kingdom of God.' According to the Bible, to inherit the kingdom of God, to receive God's blessing upon an enterprise, requires not only that the enterprise should be ethical, but that it should be run on ethical lines, if it is to bear enduring fruit.

But where, I hear you say, does that leave enterprises such as the tobacco and drinks industries, amongst the most lucrative of the twentieth century? The perspective of history will tell whether the class actions in the USA against the tobacco companies by litigious cancer sufferers will be a defining moment for the future of the enterprise. It could be that the tobacco giants are starting to reap what they have sown. Their dividends and share prices have suffered massively. There may have been a more innocent age when, before the suspected linkage between smoking and cancer, the tobacco industry could have been considered ethically good as it manufactured and sold a product that allegedly enhanced the quality of people's lives. But now when one listens to courtroom arguments by the tobacco companies that try to defend their marketing policies in full knowledge of the evidence linking smoking to lung cancer, one has to question not only the ethical stance of the company but the ethics of the lawyers who defend them. Only doing one's job is no excuse.

Oh well, I've just blown one readership market. Shall we try another now? What about the drinks industry, the producers of 'the demon drink'?

Jesus turned water into wine at the wedding feast at Cana (John 2:1-10) and Himself drank wine at the Last Supper (Matthew 26:28-29). And then Paul exhorts Timothy to drink 'a little wine' for his ailments (1 Timothy 5:23). A bit like money, all this suggests alcohol is ethically acceptable within the biblical context.

I enjoy a social drink as much as anyone, and I'm a self-confessed member of a wine club, so it must be pretty obvious that I'm not anti-alcohol or opposed to the drinks industry. I don't subscribe to the historic school of Methodism that frowns on all alcohol consumption. But I support what Methodism was trying to do in stopping the abuse that stemmed from excessive use of alcohol.

As with all enterprises, and with all human behaviour, what matters is how it is used, and if and how the industry tries to glamorise or exploit its market. Taken to extremes, alcohol abuse is as pernicious as any addiction and arguably more destructive than addiction to tobacco in the domestic and social violence it can engender. As we've seen from Galatians 5, drunkenness and debauchery are 'acts of the sinful nature'. In other words the onus switches here from the producer to the consumer of alcohol. It is the behaviour and abuse of the product that can be evil, not the product in itself. I could say something flippant here about an ethical product tasting 'evil', but let's not go there.

It all comes back to the point of a company's focus and the behaviour of the consumer. I would argue that the enterprise is ethically acceptable from a biblical standpoint, and there are many examples of drinks companies who conduct their affairs in a socially responsible way. There is, however, a real danger that a company can become unethical in the way it conducts its business or tries to develop its market.

And to get even more controversial, what about the defence industry and the mega-bucks it generates for the UK economy? Aren't they the manufacturers of weapons of mass killing and war? Is that not intrinsically evil? Don't they all fall into the hands of Hugh Laurie type characters from *The Night Manager*? Or get turned on their own people to wreak terror and despotism?

On the other hand, they can be deployed to guard freedom and can be used to fight tyranny and injustice.

I have a confession. As a consultancy we have worked with the nuclear defence industry in the UK. And we would do so again, on the grounds that their purpose is the defence and peace of the nation through deterrence. Like I say, it's complicated, isn't it?

Spirit of the enterprise

We've talked about the integrity of an enterprise and whether it can be ethical or godly. I now want to introduce the concept of the spirit of an organisation.

We have all experienced places where we feel welcome or unwelcome, where the atmosphere is light or heavy, intimate or intimidating. It is something you can't put your finger on. We often use terms like 'culture' as the catch-all to describe how a place feels, to capture the prevailing behaviours and the behaviours necessary to succeed. We use culture as a safe word to capture the intangibles and the invisible without offending political correctness by naming spiritual forces and dynamics. There are workplaces and businesses where bullying is rife or work is de-humanised, and there are workplaces where everyone is nurtured and valued as individuals for the diversity, skills, capabilities and perspective they bring.

Let me give you an example of what I mean. Think of banking and how our view of banks has been shaped by the conduct of the likes of the Royal Bank of Scotland in the years leading up the financial crash of 2007–2008. Think of the public uproar every time the subject of bankers' bonuses is raised. Is there any such thing any longer as an ethical bank? Are they all to be lumped together with the likes of RBS?

It really doesn't have to be that way. The Hancock Bank story I quoted at the beginning of this chapter and their response to disaster shows that not all banks fit the stereotype we have for them. It's a story that speaks of good management, emergency pre-planning, attention to detail and their quick implementation of recovery plans. But much more than that, it is the story of the amazing leadership of their CEO George Schloegel and COO John Hairston. When disaster struck, these men made courageous decisions based on an absolute belief in their company's purpose and identity, without regard to the risk to their business and a potential serious loss of profit.

It was what they decided to do before the Chicago facilities were online that truly shows the spirit of the organisation. In the months afterwards, overall deposits grew by $1.5 billion as new people chose Hancock Bank to be guardians of their money for the future. The spirit of the organisation, vested in the bank's leadership, courageously served the population and grew the business as a result.

There is a danger that if we think about the spiritual dynamics in organisations, we risk thinking in a binary way that commercial organisations are purely driven by the profit motive (serving mammon), and public service organisations are driven by more noble and altruistic values (serving our fellow citizens). This can lead to the popular demonisation of private enterprise without 'testing the spirits' in the way we are instructed as Christians in 1 John 4:1.

As already mentioned, we don't have to look very far to find the example of the banks and their role in the 2007–2008 economic crash. The ruthless and irresponsible push for profit exemplified by the Royal Bank of Scotland, driven by its CEO Fred Goodwin, is among the worst examples to confirm the prejudices.

What about public services such as policing or the NHS in the UK, which are not intrinsically profit driven but driven by values of social justice, protection of the vulnerable, mutual trust and equity? Or indeed the church? Does that mean there is automatically a benevolent spirit of protection, public service, care and compassion in such organisations?

In UK policing and the NHS we have sadly experienced extreme examples of what I mean by the spirit of an enterprise perverting its fundamental purposes. The police and the NHS have purposes to protect, to care and to heal. Yet the Stephen Lawrence Public Inquiry in 1998 found the Metropolitan Police Service to be institutionally racist. The 2016 Hillsborough Inquiry found the disaster to be a failure of control by the South Yorkshire Police (SYP) that had been covered up by the SYP and blamed on the behaviour of the Liverpool supporters for twenty-six years. The Stafford Hospital Public Inquiry revealed widely shocking neglect to patients in an organisation driven by its ambition to meet financial targets and become an NHS Foundation Trust. The Catholic Church, meanwhile, has been a constant focus for allegations of historical paedophilia and sexual abuse.

I don't mean to pick on the police, the NHS or the Catholic Church here. They are all highly valued, do enormous social good, and are populated by an overwhelming majority of people with great public service, faith and ethical values. My point is that these institutions comprise lots of individual organisations which are each governed by a spirit that in these extreme cases perverted their fundamental purposes.

In scripture, the book of Revelation provides a key insight to what is going on here. In Revelation the apostle John writes to the angel of the seven churches in Ephesus, Smyrna, Pergamum, Thyatira, Sardis, Philadelphia and Laodicea.

Compare, for example, the letter to the church in Ephesus with the letter to the church in Thyatira:

To the angel of the church in Ephesus write:
These are the words of him who holds the seven stars in his right hand and walks among the seven golden lampstands. I know your deeds, your hard work and your perseverance. I know that you cannot tolerate wicked men, that you have tested those who claim to be apostles but are not, and have found them false. You have persevered and have endured hardships for my name, and have not grown weary. Yet I hold this against you: you have forsaken your first love. Remember the height from which you have fallen! Repent and do the things you did at first. If you do not repent, I will come to you and remove your lampstand from its place. But you have this in your favour: you hate the practices of the Nicolaitans, which I also hate. He who has an ear, let him hear what the Spirit says to the churches. To him who overcomes, I will give the right to eat from the tree of life, which is in the paradise of God.

Revelation 2:1-7

To the angel of the church in Thyatira write:
These are the words of the Son of God, whose eyes are like blazing fire and whose feet are like burnished bronze. I know your deeds, your love and faith, your service and perseverance, and that you are now doing more than you did at first. Nevertheless, I have this against you: you tolerate that woman Jezebel, who calls herself a prophet. By her teaching she misleads my servants into sexual immorality and the eating of food sacrificed to idols. I have given her time to repent of her immorality, but she is unwilling. So I will cast her on a bed of suffering, and I will make those who commit adultery with her suffer intensely, unless they repent of her ways. I will strike her children dead. Then all the churches will know that I am he who searches hearts and minds, and I will repay each of you according to your deeds. Now I say to the rest

*of you in Thyatira, to you who do not hold to her teaching and have
not learned Satan's so-called deep secrets (I will not impose any other
burden on you): Only hold on to what you have until I come.*

Revelation 2:18-25

The spiritual environment in each of them is different. In the case
of Ephesus, they have lost their first love, while in Thyatira the issue
is tolerance of sexual immorality through the influence of Jezebel.

Note that John is not writing to the church, but to the angel of
each church. They are all churches, all seemingly sharing the same mission
and purpose, but each is distinct in its characteristics and 'spirit'.

The churches in Revelation each had their own context, history,
geography, experience, identity, culture, leadership and spirit, like a
personality of their own despite the fact they were collections of
people, each of whom were different and individual.

It is the same with organisations. Irrespective of whether they are
public sector, government, commercial, industrial, third sector or
charitable, they each have a distinct spirit and personality; their angel
if you like. And as with the churches in Revelation, that personality
and spirit evolves and changes as a living being.

If we are going to think about organisations having a personality
or spirit, we have to think of them as living and breathing entities
rather than disembodied bureaucracies or brands. We also have to
recognise that they exist within wider social systems with their own
distinctive characteristics, and are influenced by their markets and
geography. As a living entity your organisation has a personality or
spirit that shapes the way the organisation and its people operate.

And so despite all their professional regulation, training and ethical
codes of conduct, it would seem that, at the time of their respective
public scandals, the 'angels' of Mid Staffordshire NHS Foundation
Trust, the South Yorkshire Police and the Metropolitan Police, were
every bit as pernicious as the Lehman Brothers, the Royal Bank of
Scotland, or any other major financial institutions at the heart of

the recent global financial crisis.

To illustrate this at a more personal level, I want to share a couple of examples from my own experience.

Shocking though it may sound, I once worked in a hospital where the morale and reputation of staff in a specific department was at rock bottom despite its new facilities, good staffing and many excellent staff. It had been a puzzle to me for some time, as it had all the ingredients to be an excellent service with a great reputation. It started to make sense to me, however, when the HR Director told me of an informal complaint made by a member of staff about being harassed and bullied by her senior leader, who had allegedly told the staff member that whenever she thought of her, she stuck pins in a doll with her name on it!

It was never going to be easy to pursue an allegation that was effectively about witchcraft, and would doubtless be passed off by the manager as a harmless jest, but it made complete sense in identifying the spirit of witchcraft that was in play. Armed with that knowledge we were able both to pray with understanding and to investigate deeper, to the extent that we found shocking intimidation of staff through a cabal of supervisors at the next level of management, with some staff thankfully courageous enough to take a stand and tell the truth of what was happening. Effectively, good people at the supervisory level had turned into bullies through the intimidatory leadership they experienced themselves. We were able to find sufficient evidence to discipline and eventually dismiss the manager concerned. It will come as no surprise that the reputation and morale of the department concerned was subsequently transformed under new and open leadership.

On another occasion, at 4:15 pm on a Friday afternoon, my colleague Communications and Press Manager alerted me to a call from a national Sunday newspaper requesting a comment on a front-page story they were going to run that weekend about an individual's conduct in their private life that brought both their professional role and the hospital into disrepute.

The week after the story was published it became apparent that the individual's professional supervisory body had absolutely no intention of doing anything to help or support the person concerned. After months of communication, several pastoral meetings and attempts to provide support and seek resolution with the person concerned, we reached an impasse. They had no insight into the damage to their own or the hospital's reputation, and the lack of insight was compounded by inaction and seeming indifference from their professional body. Their conduct was in their private life, which meant there were no possible disciplinary actions we could take as an employer. And while I wished the person concerned no harm, I could not accept that they should continue to represent the NHS Trust I led. So I had to resort to the power of prayer to remove them from the organisation. And within no time they had got a promotion to another job!

What are we to make of this as Christians in our workplaces?

The Bible instructs us in 1 John 4:1 to 'test the spirits to see whether they are from God'. It is critical to test and discern the spirits in and of organisations. We need to discern the personality of the angel. Then, as Jesus told His disciples in Matthew 18:18, we have to use our authority as believers to loose and bind the spiritual powers at play:

Whatever you bind on earth will be bound in heaven, and whatever you loose on earth will be loosed in heaven.

In one of the examples I just quoted, I was in a position to be able to act on what I had discerned because I had positional power and there were other Christians in leadership to pray with. In the other example, it wasn't my position that secured the outcome; it was my authority as a believer.

In summary, the spirit of an organisation will be closely associated with its purpose and ethics, but its purpose does not automatically confer a beneficent spirit on the enterprise.

An ethical purpose is a great starting point, but we must be alive to the fact that even the most ethically purposed organisation can operate under a wrong spirit. That spirit could be territorial or historical and nothing directly attributable to the organisation or its leadership. Histories of social injustice, prejudice or social division can be powerful spiritual presences for enterprises in certain places. These are the things we need to discern prayerfully and with the leading of the Holy Spirit.

Not everyone will be in jobs with positional power to 'do something' and take concrete action to affect the spirit of the enterprise. But all believers at all levels of organisation are able to pray with authority regardless of their positional power. As Jesus told the seventy-two: 'I have given you authority to trample on snakes and scorpions and to overcome all the power of the enemy' (Luke 10:19). Let's all use that authority with discerning and wisdom to be the change we want to see.

So what?

If you want to apply the lessons of this book to your work life, there are several things you can do:

- Check the integrity of purpose of the enterprise you work in. Could you describe the nature of the work as pleasing, or potentially pleasing to God?

- Secondly check the integrity with which the purpose of the enterprise is being fulfilled.

- Discern the spirit of the enterprise, and pray that it will be of God, taking authority to bind and loose as your faith empowers you to do.

- Be the change you want to see – conform to the God standard for your life in your work.

- And finally, and this one makes the difference as to whether your work is *avodah* work, check whether you are fulfilling your work 'as for the Lord, not for men' (Colossians 3:23).

To re-frame those famous old lines 'It *is* what you do *and* it's the way that you do it'!

How on Earth Did That Happen?

Four

THE CLASH OF KINGDOMS
∽∾∿

H*ow come Richard never swears around you?*
(A colleague General Manager to me, referring to a peer for whom swearing was a way of life – name changed to protect possible identification.)

In chapter two I omitted to mention my fifth dragon. And this was the one that nearly blew my career. It was the dragon that said you can't be a Christian and occupy 'secular' positions of power and authority.

In the early years of my career I questioned whether a management career was compatible with my developing faith. How could I reconcile sacking someone on a Monday with the message about the love of Christ I heard on the Sunday? As well as all the enjoyable developmental stuff, how could I discipline and have to sack staff, or make people redundant to make diminishing budgets work?

I was in a real dilemma, and the truth is that I stuck with it because of the encouragement of Christian friends telling me that the world needed people in positions of influence and authority to exercise a different model of leadership from the one most of us experienced and saw at work in our daily lives.

So I kept climbing. And the more I climbed the more I found the prevailing approach of top managers to be at odds with the ethics of my faith. My career had been moving quickly, with good promotions every two or three years within the NHS. The problem was that the higher I went the greater the tension became between my faith and the culture of ambition I found around me. I had no role models to teach me how to manage and lead within a Christian framework. Well I wouldn't, would I, if I thought Christians or religious types couldn't hack it in positions of power.

There came a point in 1989 after six weeks in my first General Manager position in a large teaching hospital where I felt absolutely desperate. The responsibility felt overwhelming and some of the behaviour expected of me did not feel compatible with my beliefs and values. The learning curve demanded by the new responsibilities in a new environment was more than steep, it felt vertical! I knew that if I was going to carry on in that job and continue in a management career, it had to be on different terms to the ones that dominated the leadership culture of the organisation I worked in. I knew I couldn't compromise what I believed.

In my moment of deepest crisis one evening, after the children had gone to bed, I went to my bedroom and picked up the Bible on the bedside table. To be candid, at that stage of my life the Bible was more an ever-present ornament on the bedside table. I had tried to read it occasionally but found it impenetrable. Sitting on the edge of my bed, I just opened it randomly at Psalms. At least I thought it was randomly. Flicking through Psalms my eyes alighted on Psalm 7:8, where King David wrote:

> *Judge me, O LORD, according to my righteousness, according to my integrity, O Most High.*

In those few words I found exactly the affirmation I was seeking. All I wanted to do in my job was to do the right thing, to act honestly and with integrity. This was the standard I wanted to be judged by. And here was King David (a king no less, not just a simple hospital

General Manager!) saying it was okay. In fact, it was not just okay, it was actually God's standard. If it was good enough for a king, it had to be good enough for me! It was incredible to feel the weight and burden of the overwhelming responsibility of my new job suddenly lift from my shoulders. The God in whom I believed had lifted the burden and was telling me the way I wanted to do it was just fine. In fact, it was the way He wanted me to exercise my authority and responsibility. I had found the role model I needed. None less than King David! And for the first time in my life the Word of God had come alive to me.

But I had thought religious types couldn't hack it in positions of power and authority. This old dragon was starting to buckle at the knees. Just like the wealth thing, I began to understand that holding a position of power wasn't 'bad' or only open to ruthless and ambitious people. And exactly like the wealth thing, I started to understand it is really a matter of how power and authority are exercised that makes the difference. It's all about the heart.

So I stuck with the job. And in many respects it was the most formative period of my career precisely because it was the most adverse and difficult.

Those words from Psalm 7 were like a stamp on my soul. They lifted the weight and burden of my new responsibilities from my shoulders and told me that the way I wanted to do the job was just fine. My problem was that those standards were not, or did not appear to be, the standards of the managerial or corporate environment in which I was working. I'm not suggesting there was ever anything fraudulent or unlawful in the management ethos, but what I found most uncomfortable were the ethical and moral standards key individuals in the top leadership of the organisation modelled.

It quickly became apparent that I did not 'belong' within the informal inner circle of management and leadership of the Trust. At my first annual performance review with the Chief Executive I was told I needed to be more of a 'joiner', I needed to be more 'clubbable'.

I felt, however, I could not belong to that particular club without compromising my integrity, and in a perverse way the encouragement to become more clubbable just made me even less clubbable. I just didn't want to do key business in the pub after office hours.

I was not ashamed of my faith and wore it on my sleeve. Several of my more 'clubbable' colleagues heard the gospel, and while none gave their lives to the Lord to my knowledge at the time, some remarked how differently they behaved in my presence.

I was committed to doing the job in the best way I could. And by and large it worked. The division I managed made good progress, cracked a few intractable problems and got pretty good results.

The point came after two years in the job that I was told by a colleague that my boss wanted to get rid of me. At my third annual review, and despite good results and the award of a good performance bonus, he told me he was not going to renew my contract. I still wasn't 'clubbable'. I had to move on. He told me he didn't think I was suited to General Management or material for a Chief Executive, but I should focus on more of an advisory/expert role. And I guessed that because of my boss's wider influence and local networks, it was unlikely I could move to a Chief Executive job in the area we lived in.

That point of rejection stung as an injustice. It was the first time in my career that I had been rejected. My family was well settled and yet I knew we had to move if I was going to 'reach the top' in my career (I trust you can see me wince as I write this with hindsight!). I had been the 'golden boy' climbing the ranks at speed until then. It hurt my pride. But most importantly it opened me up to the true love of Christ. For the first time I put away my 'achiever' mask and, through the painful prospect of losing my job, I made myself truly vulnerable to receive the love of the church. And the church answered with unconditional love as only the true church of Christ can answer.

My young family was settled, we loved where we lived, we loved our church and had great friends there. But I knew my career had hit the buffers, and with hindsight it was the incentive I needed to move to the next stage of both my career and my faith. It most definitely didn't feel that way, but then again the things we need aren't necessarily the things we want or think we need at the time.

Because of the ending it didn't feel like a period of great achievement, but I was pleasantly surprised three or four years later when I met one of my former team members at a national conference and he described the period when I was in the General Manager job as the 'golden age' of the division that they looked back on fondly! God works in mysterious ways! I had considered it to be the lowest point of my career, but I also know with hindsight that it was the most formative period for my later work.

Sacred and secular

The most formative aspect of that part of my career was God's word to me from Psalm 7 at the moment of greatest crisis in my work.

Judge me, O LORD, according to my righteousness, according to my integrity, O Most High.

That was the first of many times subsequently that His word has come to my rescue.

And it was the first time I realised that God wanted me to genuinely integrate the spiritual and work sides of my life. They were not separate in His eyes.

Suddenly the church's description of things as sacred and secular made no sense at all to me. I understood that if God made me to be body, soul and spirit, then He was truly interested in every aspect of my being, not just the Sunday part.

Secular is not a word you will find in the Bible. It is a man-made separation between the seen and unseen realms of life, born in Greek philosophy as a way of making (false) sense of the world. And yet the mainstream church has perpetuated the deception, robbing many believers of their sense of vocation as a call of God rather than just a tent-making skill.

In his brilliant 2010 essay 'The Great Divide'[2], Mark Greene writes about the sacred-secular divide (SSD) and how the UK church has partially eclipsed the message of the gospel, leading to 'a narrower, less radical, less adventurous understanding of what it means to follow Jesus than the Bible's compelling picture'. Mark calls for 'a radical return to whole-life disciple-making' while recognising 'SSD has been in the church's bloodstream for nearly two millennia, and it won't give up its dominion without a fight'.

Mark's essay names the sacred-secular divide as *the* critical issue for the church to address as it permeates all church life, starting with the way we educate our children:

In fact, SSD not only affects what we teach in church, it affects our attitude to education in school. It is because of SSD that there's hardly a child or adult or youthworker who could give you a biblical perspective on maths ... It is because of SSD that Christian commentators thought long and hard about the Harry Potter novels ... and almost entirely ignored the literature our teenagers study at GCSE.

He cites the typical experience of a teacher at church:

I spend an hour a week teaching Sunday school and they haul me up to the front of the church to pray for me. The rest of the week I'm a full-time teacher and the church has never prayed for me. That says it all.

I have etched in my mind the experience of preaching one Sunday morning at a church in north-west England. As the ministry time came to an end, a man came to me with tears running down his face,

---

2 'The Great Divide', The London Institute for Contemporary Christianity, www.licc.org.uk/the-great-divide

saying that he had spent the last twenty-five years of his professional life as a social worker thinking he was a second-class Christian. But now he knew he was walking in his true vocation. He was at last free to be the social worker God had intended him to be!

If the church truly understood the nature of *avodah*, our work as worship and service to God, this sacred-secular divide would disappear in a puff of smoke, like my dragons. It would also spare my social work friend twenty-five years of pain and torment of believing he had 'copped out' from his walk with the Lord to earn his daily bread!

I pray this book can make a modest contribution to dismantling this long-standing sacred-secular divide falsehood. And set some captives free in the process.

Five

AUTHORITY AND POWER
∾◦∾

I have given you authority to trample on snakes and scorpions and to overcome all the power of the enemy; nothing will harm you.

Luke 10:19

A chapter on authority and power may seem a bit odd here when I'm supposed to be addressing the 'How on earth did that happen?' question, but it is important that we have a biblical perspective on the source of authority to be able to tell the rest of the story. It will also provide some practical biblical guidance for our workplaces and businesses. That way we can have right attitudes towards those in authority over us and also exercise authority well if we are in positions of authority and power.

Understanding the source of my authority was a critical pre-condition to the miracles God performed in my work.

As Jesus tells His disciples in Luke 10:19, Christians carry enormous spiritual authority in the places we live and work, regardless of whether we have positional power.

Paradoxically I didn't really understand that until I was in jobs with positional power. The sacred-secular dilemma I experienced in my early career was because I didn't understand my faith as giving me authority and the power of the Holy Spirit. I saw my conflict as a false struggle between compassion and mercy on the one hand, and authority and positional power on the other. In other words, I created for myself a spiritual dilemma, an 'either-or' scenario where I had to choose one or the other. God, however, sees it a different way, as an 'and-and' where positional power and the power of faith go hand in glove with one another.

Authority is something we all love to hate when other people use it overtly over us, the thing we lose respect for when it's used inappropriately, and the thing we all contest at some stage in our lives. Yet we all secretly enjoy it when we have it. We'll have a look at its twin later. Its name is 'power'. No skipping ahead allowed.

Modern day heroes often gain their status through contesting authority, through 'breaking the mould' and disturbing the order of things, through 'shifting the paradigm'. The rebel who kicks against the established order becomes the cult hero, the James Dean of the day. More often than not the passage of time ironically turns them into the new establishment as they assume authority in a world that has come to adopt their way of thinking, where the new paradigm soon becomes the new orthodoxy within the course of a generation. Some, like the Sex Pistols in the 1970s, preach anarchy and preferred death and self-destruction to conformity. Some, like James Dean, die too early to know how their lives would have turned out. Some, the majority, conform and get accused of selling out. Or maybe the reality is that they have acquired an intuitive appreciation of the concept of authority because they have understood its importance to any kind of social order and welfare in the world. For many, that's what having children does for your world-view!

Authority

Let's look at the biblical understanding of authority. It comes with a health warning that some of you may not find this comfortable. You probably won't like it or agree with it either. I know I didn't when I first discovered it. But here goes anyway.

The Bible is clear about the source of authority. It is also unequivocally clear as to how we are to behave towards those in authority. In his letter to the Romans, Paul wrote;

> *Everyone must submit himself to the governing authorities, for **there is no authority except that which God has established**.*
>
> *Romans 13:1 (emphasis mine)*

The apostle Peter was equally clear in his first letter to dispersed Christians:

> *Submit yourselves for the Lord's sake to every authority instituted among men.*
>
> *1 Peter 2:13*

We can all think of leaders and authorities whose rule over their nations have appeared abominable and offend our sense of values and justice. Surely Peter cannot have been thinking we should submit ourselves to such people? He continues:

> *Slaves, submit yourselves to your masters with all respect, not only to those who are good and considerate, but also to those who are harsh. For it is commendable if a man bears up under the pain of unjust suffering because he is conscious of God. But how is it to your credit if you receive a beating for doing wrong and endure it? But if you suffer for doing good and you endure it, this is commendable before God.*
>
> *1 Peter 2:18-20*

Wow! He really means it. Paul says every authority is *established* by God. That does not mean that every authority recognises its authority comes from God. Far from it. It would have been no more the case when Paul and Peter wrote, under the persecutory rule of the Roman Empire, than it would be today. Remember that these were not men writing in the comfort of their retirement, reminiscing about the good times with Jesus through the rose-tinted spectacles of age. These were men writing from prison or from exile, sent there by the very authorities about whom they wrote. Yet in the midst of their mal-treatment they exhorted their brethren to submit themselves to the rulers and authorities, not so they could avoid the fate they had personally suffered as some cautionary tale, but so their conduct could be 'commendable before God'.

We are also called to pray for those in positions of power:

I urge, then, first of all, that requests, prayers, intercession and thanksgiving be made for everyone – for kings and those in authority, that we may live peaceful and quiet lives in all godliness and holiness.
1 Timothy 2:1

Even though the authorities may not appreciate the source of their authority, the Bible is clear that God has established each and every authority.

Don't blame me if you find this difficult. I'm just quoting scripture.

Submission and obedience

The passages from Romans and 1 Peter beg a secondary question that should help those of you struggling with their meaning. The passages tell us to *submit*. They don't tell us to *obey*. What's the difference? The Old Testament story from Daniel 3 gives us an excellent illustration of submission to authority without obedience.

It is the story of King Nebuchadnezzar of Babylon, who made a massive gold statue and required all his subjects to bow down and worship it or else be thrown into a fiery furnace. Shadrach, Meshach and Abednego were three of his servants, of Israelite origin, who refused to worship the golden idol. When Nebuchadnezzar gives them an ultimatum to obey or die in the fiery furnace, they address him firmly but respectfully:

> '*O Nebuchadnezzar, we do not need to defend ourselves before you in this matter. If we are thrown into the blazing furnace, the God we serve is able to save us from it, and he will rescue us from your hand, O king. But even if he does not, we want you to know, O king, that we will not serve your gods or worship the image of gold you have set up.*'
>
> *Daniel 3:16-18*

It may well have been that the king was surrounded by his heavies, and I suspect most modern-day Harrison Fords would have decided they had little to lose by taking on the king and his army. After all, why go down without a fight? But no. These guys stood and addressed the man who was about to barbeque them as 'O king'. Not just once but twice! They then get thrown into the furnace apparently without a struggle. The story has a happy ending for them, of course, when they emerge unscathed and Nebuchadnezzar establishes a new law that would condemn anyone who speaks against the Israelites' God to be cut into pieces and have their houses torn down. Nice guy!

So let's not confuse submission with unfailing or unquestioning obedience. The three Israelite servants actually accept Nebuchadnezzar's authority because they accept the alternative he places before them. They don't run, fight or hide. They don't try and do a deal. They don't try and weasel their way out of it by claiming it's all a big misunderstanding. They face up to the choice they are given, and they do so respectfully. They just refuse to obey the king's command to worship the idol and compromise the integrity of their faith. Submission means accepting and respecting those placed in authority over us, but it does not imply compromising our integrity in situations where the authorities require us to do something that is clearly out of order and wrong.

Forgive me if I go all theological for a moment, but Western society also struggles with the belief that a beneficent God could establish a malevolent authority. I have lost count of the times I've heard people base their agnosticism or atheism on the premise that a loving God could not allow injustice to reign in so many situations on earth. But that's a whole different ball game that needs a separate book and a separate discussion. Suffice it to say for now that according to the Bible God created us with free will and that He does not compel anyone to do anything. To believe in Him is an active choice of will. He can certainly beat us into shape, but He never forces us into anything we don't want to do. And we can mostly track down our misfortunes when they happen to a set of choices we've made either individually or corporately, albeit occasionally passively. Remember the appeasers in the face of Hitler's threat. Happily, the Bible balances things out with the principle that rulers who abuse their authority in the eyes of God will be judged accordingly by Him:

> *Do not be deceived: God cannot be mocked. A man reaps what he sows.*
> **Galatians 6:7**

> *All who draw the sword will die by the sword.*
> **Matthew 26:52**

The central point made by Peter is when he says, 'Submit yourselves for the Lord's sake to every authority.' The submission is 'for the Lord's sake', that He might be glorified by submission to the authorities that He has established. And herein lies the rub.

For the Christian the purpose of life is to glorify God through living according to His precepts and rules. The blessing and prosperity He gives as a result is not an end in itself, it is a by-product of living a life that is 'commendable before God'.

Using authority

We've seen where authority comes from in biblical terms. Now we need to see how to use it.

In the Old Testament Joseph, David and Solomon were no less than a prime minister and two kings. They each understood the nature of their authority. They each had virtually supreme authority in their nations. They each knew to use their authority wisely (with the sad exception of Solomon in his later years). They often exercised authority in ways that were as counter-intuitive by the standards of their society as they would be by our standards today. Take Joseph's resistance to the seductive advances of his master's wife:

> *'With me in charge ... my master does not concern himself with anything in the house; everything he owns he has entrusted to my care. No-one is greater in this house than I am. My master has withheld nothing from me except you, because you are his wife. How then could I do such a wicked thing and sin against God?' And though she spoke to Joseph day after day, he refused to go to bed with her or even to be with her.*
>
> **Genesis 39:8-10**

King Saul was hunting David down to kill him, and yet when David had him at his mercy in the cave at En Gedi, he refused to allow his men to kill him, and indeed suffered remorse for simply cutting off the corner of his cloak;

> *'I will not lift my hand against my master, because he is the LORD's anointed'*
>
> **1 Samuel 24:10**

In both of these situations Joseph and David were in the preparatory phases for assuming authority and national leadership. Neither of them yet exercised the authority that was to come their way. What screams out from these episodes, however, was their intense and unshakeable respect for the men in authority over them. No matter the attractiveness of Potiphar's wife and her seductive behaviour, Joseph would not offend the integrity of his master. No matter how attractive the prospect of gaining the throne of Israel by killing the king, David would not harm Saul even though Saul was trying to kill him. In so doing David swam against the tide of opinion, in a way that was completely counter-intuitive, as his followers encouraged him to kill Saul when he had him at his mercy.

To exercise such mercy David must have had complete conviction and certainty about the integrity of his purpose and vision. While it is clear that David enjoyed great popular support for his exploits, which was one of the main causes of Saul's jealousy of him, it is not clear from the biblical accounts whether David had ambitions to be king. Nor does he ever articulate a vision for his life or his nation in the way that Joseph had done in his dreams. He seems to act, however, with a sense of purpose and personal destiny that are unshakeable and which underpin all he does. Similarly Joseph does not allow the injustice of his imprisonment to shake the vision he was given in his dreams as a young man. The way both these characters behave suggests they held firm to their sense of purpose and vision in a way that enabled them to retain the courage to swim against the tide of orthodox thinking and opinion, at the times of greatest opportunity as well as the times of most adverse pressure.

Such reverential respect for leadership nowadays is unfashionable. 'Toadying' is one of the more publishable descriptions of modern behaviour, and most people assume it's motivated by ambition for personal advancement and gain, or at the very least the desire for survival. That was not the case for either Joseph or David. Joseph was severely punished for his integrity by a long stretch in prison. David's reward was his continuing exile, persecution and pursuit by Saul.

So why did they behave in a way that ostensibly brought them punishment not reward? They did so because they did not want to offend the source of their authority. Joseph did not sleep with Potiphar's wife because he understood that offending his master in such a way was to sin against God. David didn't kill Saul because he regarded

Saul as 'the Lord's anointed'.

The last words of David, after exercising kingly power for forty years, give the key to his approach to authority and rule. They are the inspirational verses from 2 Samuel 23:

> *'When one rules over men in righteousness, when he rules in the fear of God, he is like the light of morning at sunrise on a cloudless morning, like the brightness after rain that brings the grass from the earth.'*

The standard David had asked God to judge him by was his righteousness and integrity (Psalm 7:8). At the end of his reign, surveying all he had achieved, he upheld righteousness as key in the conduct of his leadership. He also ruled 'in the fear of God'.

This 'fear of God' is not about being frightened or fearful in the contemporary sense. It is about reverence for God. Joseph and David both revered the source of their authority. Their reverence for the source of their authority meant they would exercise that authority with care, righteous diligence and with obedience.

When we look at Jesus we see He had complete knowledge of the extent of His power and authority. Yet He knew the achievement of His mission depended upon His submission to the will of the source of His authority. At the Last Supper He reveals the extent of His obedience:

> *I will not speak with you much longer, for the prince of this world is coming. He has no hold on me, but the world must learn that I love the Father and that I do exactly what my Father has commanded me.*
> ### *John 14:30-31*

Jesus' obedience extended to the laying down of His life, knowing His fate to die on the cross. He did exactly what the source of His authority told Him to do. Joseph, David and Jesus exercised enormous authority over the people of their times. But we know from the Bible narratives that they 'walked the talk'. They practised precisely what they preached. The values they espoused found life in their example. In the cases of Joseph and David they exercised formal power and authority within the governmental structure of their nations, and they led their nations into periods of great political stability and prosperity.

They did not cock a snook at authority. They understood authority in their preparatory periods to the point that they could use it discriminately and wisely when they came to power in their countries.

In summary, the key points about the biblical approach to authority and its use are:

- The Bible establishes God as the source of all authority, regardless of whether those in authority acknowledge it.
- The Old and New Testament heroes who exercised leadership authority over nations recognised the source of their authority and respected and revered those in authority over them.
- This biblical understanding of authority can lead to actions and decisions that appear counter intuitive within any historical or social context.
- Staying focused on the vision and purpose of the enterprise enables the leader to exercise the courage needed to reject the 'easy options' and swim against the tide of orthodox and popular opinion in both adverse and favourable circumstances. Painful in the short term, but far more fruitful in the long run.

What about power?

You can thank my friend Steve for this next section. After reading the section on authority in the first draft of this chapter, he asked me to explore the issue of power, which I had completely overlooked. So thank Steve and don't blame me if you get cross with this next bit!

My approach to the issue of power is from an unusual angle, but it is one with which I think we can all identify. Do you remember my first dragon, the one that was shaped by the words of the song that taught me that money was the root of all evil? How many of the things you hold as true in your life are what you learned as a child, whether for good or for bad? How many of you grew up believing you were fat, stupid, ugly, mediocre, and would never make anything in the world because someone *told* you? How many grew up believing you were handsome, bright, talented and ready to take on the world because someone *told* you. More often than not our opinions of ourselves and the world around us are shaped by what someone else has said, especially in our formative years. I don't want to go all psycho-babble on you, but you have to admit that sometimes the presence of objective evidence either to prove or disprove our beliefs about ourselves is a complete irrelevance. After all, why let the facts get in the way of a convenient life-long prejudice?

My point is that power is exercised through words and deeds. People in positions of power exercise their power through what they do and what they say. Forget about leadership power in business and enterprise for a few moments. Think about the power of a parent to shape the life of their child. Think about your own upbringing and the power your parents exercised over your emotional and intellectual development. You don't have to be a behavioural psychologist to appreciate how deeply our lives are shaped by the example and love (or absence of it) of our parents, expressed through what they said and what they did. Therapists have a whole industry based around trying to undo the damage of what someone has done or said to an individual in their formative years, and sadly many adults take the best part of a lifetime to shake off the damage done through misguided or dysfunctional parenting. Parents exercise massive power and influence over the lives of their children, often unknowingly, by what they do and what they say.

Now I am not suggesting leadership in business and service enterprise is the same as parenting. What I want to illustrate is the power of the spoken word and the power of action. In this section we're going to focus on the power of the spoken word as seen through the teaching of the Bible, and then relate it to the exercise of power in business and enterprise leadership.

Let's start with the Bible account of creation, which is based on God speaking creation into being. Theologically this is called the *Logos*, or the Creative Word. Genesis opens with the words:

In the beginning God created the heavens and the earth. Now the earth was formless and empty, darkness was over the surface of the deep, and the Spirit of God was hovering over the waters. And God said, 'Let there be light,' and there was light.

Genesis 1:1-3

There then follow a further five occasions in Genesis 1 where the following pattern is repeated:

And God said, 'Let ...' And it was so.

Thus, in the biblical account God creates the sky, the land, vegetation, the stars, and the living creatures of the air, sea and land simply by speaking them into existence.

In Proverbs 18:21, Solomon captures the power of the spoken word and the power of the tongue dramatically and succinctly:

The tongue has the power of life.

Moving into the New Testament, the most eloquent passage on the power of the tongue and the spoken word is found in James 3:

When we put bits into the mouths of horses to make them obey us, we can turn the whole animal. Or take ships as an example. Although they are so large and are driven by strong winds, they are steered by a very small rudder wherever the pilot wants to go. Likewise the tongue is a small part of the body, but it makes great boasts. Consider what a great forest is set on fire by a small spark. The tongue is also a fire, a world of evil among the parts of the body. It corrupts the whole person, sets the whole course of his life on fire, and is itself set on fire by hell ... With the tongue we praise our Lord and Father, and with it we curse men, who have been made in God's likeness. Out of the same mouth come praise and cursing. My brothers, this should not be. Can both fresh water and salt water flow from the same spring? My brothers, can a fig-tree bear olives, or a grapevine bear figs? Neither can a salt spring produce fresh water.

James 3:3-12

The tongue, the spoken word, can create and it can also destroy. How many of your dreams have been enabled or destroyed by the word on someone's tongue? In Britain during the Second World War there was a saying that 'careless talk costs lives'. You may not be working in an enterprise or business that deals in life or death, but the careless word in any of our working environments can have potentially massive and often unintended consequences. It makes you think we should all be born with a little label on our tongues that says 'use with care'.

What does this mean for working in business and enterprise? Whether you are a positional leader or not, it means that power can be exercised either creatively or destructively through what you say and do. It means your words have to be carefully framed and chosen in full knowledge of the impact they can have on your listener, and even on their unintended audiences. That responsibility is especially great if you are a leader or carry management responsibilities.

We readily appreciate the oratory of great leaders, but only rarely do most leaders appreciate the power of their words to create and motivate amongst their followers. David and Solomon were both kings and enjoyed the constitutional power given by their positions. They were also great writers who conveyed their sense of purpose and leadership through what they wrote.

David was the equivalent of a modern Nobel Prize winner for the quality of his poetry, and the lyrical wisdom of Solomon in his proverbs must have been at least as influential to his contemporary audiences as David's writing had been for his.

We so often think of those in positions of power as driven by ambition and power-lust, but who can forget David's description of the righteous leader as 'like the light of morning at sunrise on a cloudless morning, like the brightness after rain that brings the grass from the earth' (2 Samuel 23:4)?

Both David and Solomon used the written word as a vehicle to convey their leadership messages and beliefs. Clearly the circumstances were different culturally from the environment of communications saturation we 'enjoy' today. Indeed, the modern-day British citizen might look slightly askance if the Prime Minister or the Queen chose to convey their key messages to the nation through the medium of poetry. My point is (just in case you've missed it) that leadership can exercise power and shape the beliefs and action of their community of followers by the written word as well as by the spoken word.

Whatever the leader says, however, will be of little value if it isn't backed up by coherent and consistent action in the exercise of power. How did our Old Testament heroes do when it came to exercising their power?

Of course they weren't perfect. David messed up and abused his power when he engineered the death in battle of Bathsheba's husband. Fortunately he saw the error of his ways and it wasn't terminal for his kingship or his nation. Solomon got rather carried away in later life with his obsession with women, and unfortunately that was terminal for the long-term health of the nation he led because he didn't make it good and he continued to dishonour the source of his authority until his death. But the overall picture is that during their kingships they use their power with integrity and wisdom. A marvellous example with Solomon is his ruling over the disputed ownership of a baby:

Now two prostitutes came to the king and stood before him. One of them said, 'My lord, this woman and I live in the same house. I had a baby while she was there with me. The third day after my child was born, this woman also had a baby. We were alone; there was no-one in the house but the two of us. During the night this woman's son died because she lay on him. So she got up in the middle of the night and took my son from my side while I your servant was asleep. She put him by her breast and put her dead son by my breast. The next morning I got up to nurse my son – and he was dead! But when I looked at him closely in the morning light, I saw that it wasn't the son I had borne.' The other woman said, 'No! The living one is my son; the dead one is yours.' But the first one insisted, 'No! The dead one is yours; the living one is mine.' And so they argued before the king ... Then the king said, 'Bring me a sword.' So they brought a sword for the king. He then gave an order: 'Cut the living child in two and give half to one and half to the other.' The woman whose son was alive was filled with compassion for her son and said to the king, 'Please, my lord, give her the living baby! Don't kill him!' But the other said, 'Neither I nor you shall have him. Cut him in two!' Then the king gave his ruling: 'Give the living baby to the first woman. Do not kill him; she is his mother.' When all Israel heard the verdict the king had given, they held the king in awe, because they saw that he had wisdom from God to administer justice.

1 Kings 3:16-28

Solomon held the power of life and death in his hands, but we can see from this example how creatively he used his words and wisdom to arrive at the truth in an incredibly delicate situation. And all without the assistance of DNA sampling!

Solomon's greatest desire at the beginning of his kingship was to be given wisdom to rule and lead the people (2 Chronicles 1:10). He understood the connection between power and wisdom. In Proverbs 24:5 he wrote:

A wise man has great power.

When the people of Israel heard of his ruling over the disputed baby 'they held the king in awe'. How would you like to be held in awe by the people you lead? Or hold your workplace leaders in awe because of their wisdom?

Let's turn to Joseph and see how he exercised his power. He was effectively the prime minister of one of the world super-powers of the time, and he happened to have the added advantage of ruling in the only country around that had any stock-piles of food during the seven years of famine that struck that region of the world. Just think of the power and influence wielded today by the leadership of a nation that was sitting on the only viable stock-pile of oil or gas in the modern world during a seven-year oil famine. Quite a nice position to be in if you want to pull off some juicy international deals and establish a position of global influence. Add to that the fact that part of this leader's early life education had been his betrayal and sale into slavery by his brothers, and we not only have a picture of potential global dominance by this individual but the added spice of having the power to avenge himself of the injustices he had suffered at the hands of his own family. Real blockbuster material for the big screen or an epic novel. But what did Joseph do?

His brothers came to Egypt to buy food and he had them at his mercy, even though they did not recognise him. Two passages from Genesis encapsulate his response in his position of great power. The first comes as he identifies himself to his brothers:

'I am your brother Joseph, the one you sold into Egypt! And now, do not be distressed and do not be angry with yourselves for selling me here, because it was to save lives that God sent me ahead of you.'
Genesis 45:4-5

The second comes as his brothers throw themselves on his mercy after the death of their father:

His brothers then came and threw themselves down before him. 'We are your slaves,' they said. But Joseph said to them, 'Don't be afraid. Am I in the place of God? You intended to harm me, but God intended it for good to accomplish what is now being done, the saving of many lives. So then, don't be afraid. I will provide for you and your children.' And he reassured them and spoke kindly to them.

Genesis 50:18-21

Here there is no gratuitous use of power. No revenge. No pay-back time. No deals. Just love and compassion, underpinned by an understanding of the bigger picture in which all the history of their relationship had been played out. Could you picture this scene today, where the monopolistic oil baron forgives and forgets the debts and wrongs of the very people who sold him down the river into slavery and subsequently into the misery of prison, to invite them to come and live with him to share the good of his abundance? Not quite in the script of a James Bond movie, is it?

Now it may be that after due consideration you would still prefer to enjoy your transient moment of triumph by settling old scores with your adversary of all these years, instead of establishing an enduring model of leadership and sticking to the vision and purpose of what you're doing. It may be that the hit-list you've saved up all these years for when you get into that position of power is just too woven into the fabric of your being to give up that easily.

But if that's you, and I really don't want to spoil your fun, I'm afraid you're reading the wrong book.

Authority and power go hand in hand, and what we see with our Old Testament leadership examples is that their understanding of the source of their authority influences dramatically the way they exercise their power. By any measure they had far more legitimate power than either you or I could ever dream of exercising, but by honouring the source of their authority they hold to the trust that has been placed in them, and they hold to the vision and purpose inherent in that trust.

To summarise what we learn about power from the Bible:

- Power is to be exercised within the framework created by the source of authority.
- There is incredibly creative or destructive power in the words leaders use to express themselves. Use that power with care! Even if they don't cost lives, careless words can create havoc in any enterprise. 'The tongue has the power of life.'
- Power is not only expressed through what leaders say but also through what they do.
- Great power is exercised through wisdom. 'A wise man has great power.'

So what?

What do we take away from this biblical perspective on authority and power as far as our workplace and businesses are concerned?

- We are all called to pray for our leaders, whether they are believers or not, harsh or compassionate, gifted or incompetent. Hard I know, but nothing is impossible for God and, whether or not the leader changes as a result of our prayer, God sees our heart. And He will hold me accountable for my heart, not my pastor or my parents. And He will hold you accountable for your heart, not your spouse or your neighbour or your boss. Simple as that.

- We are also called to submit to our leaders, but scripture shows how we should distinguish this from obedience if we are asked to perform unrighteous tasks.

- If you are not a leader or hold a management position, you could become that leader one day – neither Joseph nor David showed ambition to lead their nations, but their attitude of heart and submission to authority was fundamental to their trust-worthiness before God.

- If you are a leader, you are most certainly called to exercise your leadership from a biblical understanding of your responsibilities.

- As believers we have to choose and use our words carefully because they carry immense creative and destructive power.

THE AXE-MAN!

∞∞

Blessed are you when people insult you, persecute you and falsely say
all kinds of evil against you because of me. Rejoice and be glad,
because great is your reward in heaven.

Matthew 5:11-12

In chapter three I told you about my fateful performance review where I was told my contract would not be renewed and how my boss thought I was not Chief Executive material.

Within six months, in 1992, I was appointed to my first Chief Executive job in the south-east of England.

We saw in the last chapter that Joseph, David and Solomon were no corporate lightweights. They led their nations with political and commercial acumen. Joseph made hard-headed decisions in his handling of the food stocks in the period of famine, to the extent that the people of the country were prepared to commit themselves into bondage to Pharaoh. David conquered his enemies and led his nation to a level of prosperity and peace they had never known. Solomon clearly had a flair for exploiting foreign brains and foreign skills and turning them to his own advantage so the basically peasant regime of his father

David developed Israel by leaps and bounds into a first-class economic powerhouse.

It is also true to say that the Bible records the fortunes of a few kings of Israel who totally blew their responsibilities. You can read 1 and 2 Kings for yourself if you want to follow the historical peaks and troughs of the nation of Israel, but what is absolutely clear from the biblical accounts is how inextricably linked the fortunes of the nation are with the conduct of its kings and their relationship with God.

The rubber hits the road

After the Lord's word to me in 1989 about righteousness and integrity, it's fair to say that when I took up my first role as a CEO, my understanding of the spiritual reality of leadership meant that I knew I was accountable to God for what I did and I wanted my work to be acceptable to Him.

This was a time when the NHS saw the introduction of an 'internal market' in healthcare where, theoretically at least, the best would flourish and weakest would go to the wall. My experience in my previous job had given me only limited exposure to corporate political life and, truth be told, I was not equipped to discern fully just how promising (or otherwise) the circumstances were that I was going into. The Chairman, who came into her job about fifteen months after me, later told me she was warned off it as a 'poisoned chalice' Trust that was set up to fail. It didn't fail. On the contrary, it positively flourished in the environment of the time. But not without having to face head-on some of what are now euphemistically described as 'challenges'.

I was not universally welcomed as the new face of NHS leadership. The local newspaper's health correspondent warned me on first meeting that she had been briefed to give me a hard time, but I decided, nonetheless, to relate to her with honesty and openness from the outset. As a result I gained her respect and, despite her editorial instruction, she went on to report me accurately and fairly whenever we spoke. I know that early transparency stood me in good stead later on when she was able to correct quite personal public criticism of me because of what I had said to her on the record when we first met.

Indeed, I soon found myself the subject of speculative and misleading comment in the local newspaper by an outspoken local politician. I had to choose whether and how to respond to the adverse and occasionally personal comment. I chose to stay silent around the allegations and not to respond in kind. There was nothing to be gained from rising to the goading other than escalating it.

I discovered pretty soon after starting the job that the organisation had rather shakier financial foundations than I had been led to believe. I had arrived in June and there were no budgets set and no healthcare contracts signed for the financial year beginning the previous 1 April. No way to run a business! We had a brand-new hospital with several empty wards because there wasn't enough money to staff them.

The first performance report I received from my new Director of Finance after he arrived was that we were nearly £1m in deficit after five months of the year on a turnover of £42 million. The financial disciplines were such that while NHS Trusts were not allowed to make 'profits', as a public body we were required to break-even year-on-year. The 'challenge', therefore, was not only to recover the deficit already incurred during the year, but to reduce on-going expenditure to live within the means of the expected income for the following year.

For those of you with a Health Service or wider public service background, I'm conscious I'm going to focus here on the money side of things, which risks confirming your worst fears that all CEOs ever think about is the money. Not so – but I also have a basic belief that organisations, just like people in everyday life, have to take responsibility for their finances to be able to keep their freedom to make choices. When you lose control of your money, you give someone else the power to make choices over your future.

When re-structuring the management of the organisation the first appointment we had made was Director of Finance. While I didn't know it at the time, we appointed a born-again Christian called Chris. Independently of one another we had been praying about what was needed to get the finances in order. Once we discovered our mutual faith we joined together in prayer about what we should do. I also had a lot of prayer support from my wife and my local church pastor, seeking godly solutions to the difficulties.

There followed eighteen months of dramatic financial re-structuring, all in the public eye and extremely contentious. The closure of a much-loved community hospital, ward closures, and a programme of staff redundancies and management re-structuring took place. It was a tough programme but it worked, and got the organisation into a strong position to be able to develop its services. It would certainly not have seemed to the outside world that our programme of action was based on prayer, but it was. It was also based on my sense of personal responsibility before God to take leadership in a difficult set of circumstances rather than pass the buck for someone else to sort out. In that regard, though I didn't realise it at the time, I was setting something in place about the spirit of the organisation to take responsibility for itself and find our own solutions.

Suddenly I found myself taking precisely the kind of decisions that I had previously considered incompatible with Christianity. I was making people redundant and even found some of them thanking me for my honesty and the fact that I was prepared to deal with them and see them personally. I won't pretend they all took it that way, but the process was actually really humbling. How was such action compatible with my faith, when I was ostensibly taking away people's careers and livelihoods, and when my actions were causing massive local disturbance publicly?

I quickly acquired the title of 'axe-man'. I had my cartoon face on the front page of the local newspaper two weeks in a row, wielding an axe with blood coming from my mouth. On one occasion a packed public meeting was convened in a church hall, and the local newspaper showed a photograph of an empty seat on the platform with my name on it – the seat was empty because I didn't know the meeting was happening and I had not been invited. Colleagues in the hospital found a Guy Fawkes dummy with my name on it in a meeting room. And so on ...

I had a very difficult meeting with the editor of the newspaper at my request, where he made it obvious to me that I was fair game for public vilification if it helped his circulation, regardless of the merits of the case for change.

I may not have been getting everything right, and the results were painful for many people, but I knew that I was trying to do my job with righteousness and integrity. Everything we did was based in prayer, and when each challenge arose in the three years between 1992 and 1995 I had an answer and a clear course of action to take. I believe those courses of action were given to me by God in answer to prayer. I don't say this to try and minimise in any way my personal responsibility for the impact of the actions we took. I stood up very clearly and publicly for what was being done, however unpopular and uncomfortable it may have been, and I didn't offer the 'answer to prayer' or 'it's all God's fault' responses. I tried to fulfil my accountability honestly, with integrity and openness. I tried to give honest answers to honest questions.

But those close to me, especially my wife, my pastor and Chris, the Director of Finance, all knew what we were doing was implementing the answers God had given me in prayer.

Moving up the faith gears

After two very hard years initially, my third year in the job was relatively comfortable.

The first two years had created a solid financial foundation on which we could develop our healthcare services locally. The tough decisions had all been taken in that period. 1994/5 had its challenges, too, but they were never so serious and it was really the year in which we started to build.

We had ended each of the previous years in good financial shape. We had prayed for management answers to getting the money issues sorted out and they had been given, and they had worked. It all served to confirm the Bible teaching that God really was interested in every aspect of my life.

Having felt as though I'd been thrown into the deep end two years earlier, now it felt like I was swimming. I had a full management team in place, including another of the directors who was a born-again Christian. Believe me, we did not appoint directors with a prior knowledge of their faith, but it could be no coincidence that there was now a core of Christians in the Trust's leadership.

By the beginning of my fourth year we thought the major financial challenges were behind us because the previous year had been relatively comfortable. So when we found ourselves in August 1996 with a deficit of £360,000 after only three months of the financial year it came as a major shock.

In the 'internal market' years of the early and mid-1990s NHS Trusts were run on quasi-commercial grounds ('quasi' because they remained public bodies) whereby income had to be 'earned' for work done via contracts for service and something like 25–30 per cent of the Trust's income (in our case about £15 million a year) was uncertain and volatile. The theory was that Trusts got paid for what they did, that money would follow patients' choices about where to receive their healthcare, that the better hospitals and Trusts would be rewarded to develop their services through improved market share, and that the less effective Trusts would have to shape up to the competition or go to the wall. The theory was fine, but it also assumed that the 'purchasers' of the healthcare had unlimited funds to pay for the extra 'volume of care' given by Trusts, which was of course not the case in a politically-led taxation-funded and cash-limited system.

So there we were. Three months into a new financial year,

£360,000 in the red. Our contracts were 'over-performing' (forgive the quasi-commercial jargon). In other words, we were doing more work than we were being paid for, about 5–6 per cent more than our purchasers were prepared to 'buy'. Chris and I had to go to the Board with a set of proposals to get the income and activity back into balance. Not only because it made 'business sense', but because as a public body we had a legal duty to break-even on our income and expenditure.

And while I may not have liked the fact we had such a duty, it was my responsibility to ensure we observed the legal duties placed upon us by Statute. Back to the submission thing!

So we examined the reasons behind the deficit and the 'over-performance' in activity, and we looked at the options to reduce the activity. We knew we could not go to the Board with a proposal just to let the activity continue and hope we'd get somewhere in negotiating additional income. We knew that a deficit equivalent to £120,000 a month meant the best part of £1.5 million in a year, and we also knew from experience that handling that kind of deficit could not be done without re-structuring the very services we were now set on building. So we looked at the options to re-structure services and we prayed. And we looked again. And we prayed again. And we kept on looking and we kept on praying. But this time God did not seem to be responding to our prayers. Our hearts sank at the prospect of having to re-visit the financial 'cuts' approach of previous years, and neither Chris nor I had any peace about curtailing services in the way we had done previously.

Fortunately we did not have a Board meeting scheduled in August so we didn't have to go to the Board that month with a proposed set of solutions. We did, however, keep the Board appraised informally and chose to follow a line of 'keeping our nerve' and re-invigorating 'internal discipline and control' so the situation could not deteriorate. What that really meant was that we had not got a clue what to do and we did not believe that curtailing patient care services was the answer.

Enter the prophetic

And then the answer came, but in a way that was completely different to all our previous experience. Whereas the hallmark of the previous years had been 'management solutions' to prayer, this was to be the start of a series of 'spiritual' solutions. Miracles. This is where the ride may get really bumpy for any sceptics among you, but hang in there and enjoy the fun. You never know, you may even discover a source of renewal that would radically change your approach to business.

My family and I are members of Kingdom Faith Church in Horsham. In those days the church held both morning and evening meetings every Sunday, both lasting two to three hours. We always attended the morning family service, but as we live some distance from the church and had three young children it wasn't so easy to attend the evening meetings. Occasionally, however, I would feel the urge to go, maybe once every couple of months. And one such Sunday evening the preacher was a guy called Richard Roberts, the son of a famous American 'father of the faith' Oral Roberts, who had founded a Christian university in the USA.

Richard told of how he had taken over from his father as the university CEO when the organisation's finances were looking a bit bleak. He didn't know just how perilous the position was until he really got his feet under the desk. Not long in post he discovered the debt was in the order of $20 million and the banks were threatening closure on all lines of credit, etc. He soon came under heavy pressure to sell one of the university's buildings that had been on the market for several years at a valuation of around $3 million. They had not previously found a buyer but suddenly one had appeared and was offering the market price.

In the meantime, Richard had discovered early in his tenure that the university's finance department had stopped its corporate tithing. In Malachi 3 the Bible says that the first tenth of everything belongs to the Lord and the Israelites had 'robbed' God by stopping their tithing. God's promise in Malachi 3 is that if they will restore the tithe He will open the windows of heaven to bless them. Well some diligent accountant had decided that with the university's finances being in such a perilous state it was only logical that they could not give away a tenth of their income when they were in such debt. Richard immediately restored the tithe, the banks went ape, and the rest is history. He tells the story in full in his book *The Joy of the Lord*, but I'm just giving you the highlights as he told it that night (or at least how I heard it).

To cut a long story short the deficit was cut by $12 million in a single year through a dozen unsolicited gifts of around $1million each, and the property valued at $3 million was eventually sold for $6 million!

I listened to him completely and utterly entranced. If tithing could do that for a debt of $20 million then I reckoned £360,000 should be easy. I knew this was God's message for me, the answer to our prayer, but I hadn't got a clue how it could be done in an NHS Trust where it would have been illegal to tithe a tenth of our income in the way Richard had described. We simply could not act that way in a publicly tax-funded system.

First thing the following Monday morning I went to Chris's office and shared with him what I had heard. I added that I just couldn't see how we could do the same. Chris looked at me and instantly replied, 'Then maybe what we can do is tithe our work. We'll cut nothing but do more than we're paid for.' Bear in mind that this man was the Trust Director of Finance, the man whose job security depended on delivering the financial targets and results set by the Board. The man whose job was to make sure the bottom line balanced. The man with whom I had been discussing options to curtail services. The man who had backed me through the tough early years to get the organisation into hard-won financial order.

The man who had often faced the opprobrium of the staff and the public because he constantly reminded us of the need to balance the books whatever the price. And here he was responding instantly that we should close nothing but, if anything, accelerate the rate at which we were 'over-performing' our contracts when there was no sign of a financial settlement on the horizon anywhere from anyone.

And I knew straight away from the witness in my spirit that he was right. The Holy Spirit had spoken!

We shared the strategy with our colleague Stefan, Director of Business Development. After all it was his job to get the money in, so quite apart from his own faith perspective, Chris and I reckoned he should have the opportunity to pray it through as well. He thought it was the right way forward too, but how on earth could we sell such a strategy to the Board when we had always had such a strong focus on disciplined financial management? How, for example, would the non-executive director who was the ex-MD of an international bank react to such a plan?

By God's grace there wasn't a Board meeting in August, so we didn't have to go and seek their agreement. Instead we decided the prudent course was to stick with the 'hold our nerve' line until the September Board. Our record was such that the Board had confidence in the combined judgement of the CEO and FD and they backed us without too many problems.

What about our integrity? The truth is that we felt we couldn't go to the Board promoting a 'faith' answer ahead of producing results. We also knew as experienced Board directors in our own right that we had to allow the Board to review the position on a month-by-month basis.

By the October Board meeting the situation had started to turn the right way after the deficit actually stabilised in August. By the end of November Stefan was able to report contract increases of £750,000 from two of our principal purchasers. Such mid-year increases were unprecedented from either of the health authorities concerned. They had a history of never agreeing additional contract income during the course of the year until the last quarter (i.e. January–March) and they were both agreeing significant new sums of cash early in the third quarter of the year. Our cost-per-case income (the 'volatile' £15 million a year) started to increase and exceed our income targets.

By December Chris was reporting to the Board that the income and expenditure position was moving into balance and yet our contracts, despite the new income agreed with the purchaser health authorities and GP fundholders, continued to exceed even the adjusted targets.

In mid-January of 1996 Chris came to see me with the draft financial results for December. He told me we had a problem and didn't know what to do. Things had not quite worked out the way he expected. I braced myself for the bad news. He then told me we had a projected surplus of £1 million and he didn't know how we could handle it! Remember the context. We were a public body unable to make profits and with very little leeway to carry surpluses forward. Yet here we were, only eleven weeks away from the end of the financial year and we had too much money!

With what I can only describe as the joy of the Lord, and guided by the Holy Spirit, we started making plans there and then to spend the money by cutting waiting lists for patients, buying new equipment we had previously been unable to afford, replacing outdated medical and diagnostic equipment. We even decided to pay all staff a flat-rate bonus which was something virtually unheard of in the NHS. Consultant medical staff and domestic staff alike received the same bonus of £75. It wasn't a lot, but it was a concrete way of saying 'thank you' to all staff regardless of status or grade. Whisper it, but the truth is that we did no financial calculations regarding affordability. We prayed, landed on some figures and acted on them.

Believe it or not it's actually quite difficult to spend a surplus £1 million in eleven weeks in a responsible and accountable way to benefit patient care, but we managed to put together a set of proposals the Board supported wholeheartedly.

And the result? The audited accounts for the Trust for 1995/96 showed a small surplus of £3,000! Not only had the deficit been recovered but we had invested an additional unplanned £1 million in the last two months of the year.

'But what about the tithe?' I hear you ask.

The spiritual answer had been to tithe our work. That year we exceeded our contracts, after the adjustments to take account of the contract changes, by 9 per cent on in-patients, 11 per cent on day cases and 10 per cent on out-patient work. All without charge. We didn't plan the over-activity in any deliberate or rational way. We couldn't have conjured up new work even if we had wanted to. There's actually not a lot you can do to manage the activity figures so accurately or responsively. Those figures were simply the result of that decision to obey God, tithe our work and carry on doing what we believed the organisation was there to do, which was to provide patient care to those in need as quickly as possible. And at the end of it all we were able to give a little something back to the staff as a 'thank you' that was appreciated by all precisely because it did not differentiate between any of them.

Explain that away!

We decided the 'how did you do it?' questions were best handled informally and mostly on a one-to-one basis, though not exclusively so.

When we shared it with the whole senior management team of nine at one of our weekly meetings there were doubters, though remarkably some non-believers got closer to believing the story than some believers. It sometimes never ceases to amaze me how we Christians can limit God!

I had a couple of remarkable conversations with non-executive directors of the Board. Two of them cornered me after a Board meeting and demanded to know the real story of how we turned the situation around. When I told them the full story, they responded immediately by talking about how they could tithe work in their own professional and business lives through pro-bono work! When I recounted the full story to my Chairman at the end of my annual review meeting she responded calmly that she believed all I had said, but was going to give the performance bonus to me rather than to the Lord!

There were many other occasions, including at the Trust's annual review with the NHS Executive, when we shared the 'real story' and our NHS Executive colleague responded that his brother was a minister and had been trying to get him to give his life to the Lord for years! There were moments of jaw-dropping silence around the table, but never followed by dismissal. I learned many years later that a Health Authority Chief Executive was privately trying to encourage other Trusts to follow our lead. By and large the people we were dealing with knew us also from the hard years and we had credibility with them in a way that meant they would take seriously what we said.

How on earth did that happen?

The observant among you will have spotted that, at a purely rational business level, we got into trouble by doing more work than we were paid for. And we then got out of trouble by … doing more work than we got paid for!

So how does that work? How can the solution be identical to the problem?

The answer is two-fold.

Firstly, the solution came from hearing God, however counter-intuitive it may have been in business terms. Both Chris and I had the witness of the Spirit as confirmation. It wasn't simple escapism, avoiding the difficult choices we had taken in previous years.

Secondly, it was a matter of our hearts:

The LORD does not look at the things man looks at. Man looks at the outward appearance, but the LORD looks at the heart.

1 Samuel 16:7

Both of us knew that we knew the Lord had spoken. The Lord knew our hearts to trust Him and serve Him in our work and He rewarded us accordingly.

Perseverance in faith

... but the LORD looks at the heart

To be honest, the most difficult moment for me came when I was invited to speak to Kingdom Faith Church about the miracle. We were now in July 1996 and the invitation had come in response to my sharing the tithing episode with the church's senior pastor.

As I stood up in front of several hundred people one Sunday morning, the difficult thing wasn't sharing the episode so that God could be glorified, it was because the previous week I'd received the financial results for the first two months of the new financial year.

After the events of the previous year we believed that tithing our work was the answer and strategy for the Trust. We hadn't bothered to check it out with the Lord – we just felt it was an obvious thing to do based on the miracle of the previous year. And here we were, £220,000 in the red after only two months of the new financial year, and this time we weren't doing more work than we were paid for.

I had wrestled with whether I should go ahead with my testimony in the light of the latest position, but I put the doubts behind me because I couldn't allow this setback to undermine the miracle God had worked. In every way this was the most public declaration I could make. But what if I ended up with egg on my face through a publicly visible financial disaster in the new year? That old pride thing rearing up again!

And that's where my next step of faith had to be. I was not going to deny what God had done; I was determined to glorify Him for His faithfulness to that promise from Malachi 3, so that's what I did.

By mid-July Chris had reported pretty awful results for June. The deficit had more than doubled in the month of June and the tithing of activity still didn't seem to be working either. After three months the new-year overspend was the worst since my very first year in the job, £465,000, and activity was pretty much on target so we had no case for pursuing and negotiating more income or for fooling ourselves that we were tithing again.

As in the previous year we had prayed for an answer and it hadn't come. In fact, things were worse. Yet we knew the 'old' solutions of cutting capacity and embarking on further major savings programmes was not the answer. Just as an aside and as further background, all of this took place in a national climate where we were required to reduce costs by 3 per cent every year anyway (about £1.5 million a year at that time) in order to produce a balanced budget, so simple 'efficiencies' would actually have meant real cuts in healthcare provision. It was a policy introduced by Government in the early 1980s as an annual 1 per cent, and ran at around 3 per cent for most of the 1990s.

I didn't know where to turn except to God. For four consecutive years we had balanced our finances and developed patient care services locally to high standards. We couldn't turn back now. One early morning at home, in my daily 'quiet time', I asked the Lord for something in prayer I had never dared ask before. I asked Him to tell me what the July financial position was, just so I could be sure His hand was still on my work. Instantly a figure came into my mind of £372,000. I am not so super-spiritual as to believe that every thought I have in times of prayer is actually God speaking to me, but I am spiritual enough to know He can do things like that when we least expect and that the experience is rarely like Moses' burning bush or accompanied by fanfares of angels. It just appears and you know that you know.

The Bible teaches that the way to distinguish our own thoughts from God's voice is to 'test the spirits', and so I decided to do just that. I went into the office. It was a Friday. I went to see Chris to ask if he had the July results yet. He said he didn't. He was waiting to get the draft results later that day. I told him I did have the results, and that the deficit had reduced to £372,000. He looked at me quizzically and asked how I knew. I told him God had told me when I asked in prayer. While £372,000 wasn't great, it was a lot better than the previous month. Chris politely stayed quiet but I knew he was thinking I had finally lost the plot.

About 6.00 p.m. that Friday Chris came to my office saying he wanted to discuss with me the draft results he had just received. He said there was good news and bad news. The bad news was that the deficit had gone up; the good news was that the rate of deterioration had slowed down!

We then spent half an hour reviewing each of the income and expenditure lines at summary level, against which I made a number of comments. He said he would get his team to do further work on Monday before the results were published. I didn't mention the £372,000 figure again, but I didn't believe the draft figures Chris had given me, and all through the weekend I was certain of the improvement.

Come Monday I didn't trouble Chris again until late afternoon. I went to his office and he was meeting with his deputy. I asked if he had the results yet. He said they were literally finalising them in their meeting, but had already made some adjustments. I asked if I could listen in and took a seat. Chris' deputy then turned to him and said, 'Roger was right about the fundholding income line, we under-estimated it by £86,000.' Chris said, 'Okay, £86,000 more income brings us down from £458,000 to …' and he tapped the figures into his calculator. I instantly said £372,000. He looked at me, eyes wide open and said, 'I'd forgotten that!' His jaw dropped. His poor deputy didn't know what on earth was going on between us. So we told her. God's interest in our affairs was such that He knew our financial results well before we did.

I assume you can now picture how the rest of the year went. There were no massive new sources of income coming in, but gradually the deficit decreased. We again finished the year on 31 March 1997 almost exactly in balance on a budget of about £50 million.

How on earth did that happen?

I had personally gone through three significant tests of my faith. The first happened when I had to get up in front of my church and testify to God's miracle in our finances in July 1996 in the full knowledge that the circumstances were once again pretty bleak. The second was holding on to the certain knowledge that God's hand was on my work despite the worsening circumstances in August that year. The third was the absolute peace and certainty I had that Friday evening and all the following weekend after Chris had given me the bad news about the draft results for July. I trusted God on each occasion to overcome the circumstances, and that's exactly what He did. I am not claiming some incredible prophetic gift that allows me to know my organisations' results as some matter of routine long before they happen. That was the only time I have ever asked God to let me know our financial position and He answered me because He knew my heart and how troubled I was, and how desperately I was holding onto His promise, the promise that my enterprise would prosper. He gave me the prophetic answer when I needed it most. It was the second successive year in which God had given a spiritual solution to a business problem.

Why had the spiritual answers been different between the two years? I don't know and God hasn't told me. I do know, however, that I learned not to assume there are standard 'mechanical' spiritual answers to business problems. We had gone into 1996/7 assuming tithing was the answer as it had been the previous year. I know I didn't ask or seek God specifically on the subject, I just assumed what God had blessed one year He would bless again the next. It wasn't that I didn't pray. I did. But I didn't ask or seek the answer. I just assumed it. That experience taught me never to assume the answer from God but to seek it. Tithing our work was the answer for one year and for the next year the answer was a prophetic word of knowledge. On each occasion the test of faith was holding to the prophecy.

Obedience and vindication

The stories I have just told show God working for the corporate welfare of the organisation I worked in. But He wasn't only interested in our finances. He was also interested in my reputation.

I wrote earlier of my experience at the hands of the local press and a specific local politician, who took every opportunity they could to undermine my reputation, including engineering the church hall public meeting with my name on the empty chair.

I had been in the job for five years, and while the editor of the local paper had moved on (and his replacement was more amenable to open and fair coverage of our work), the local politician continued to harangue me publicly at every opportunity, including an allegation in the name of whistle-blowing to *World in Action*, ITV's investigative documentary programme. As with previous allegations I gave the press open access and answered the allegations directly in a recorded interview on national TV. As with previous allegations the issue then went away, never to appear again, and no formal whistle-blowing complaint was ever lodged.

And yet in those five years the only conversations the councillor and I had ever had were across crowded public meeting rooms. We had never met one to one.

With that context I'm sure you will understand if I use made-up names for this next story. The corporate stories are all verifiable in terms of the results, but this one is very personal to all involved and you will have to take me on trust.

One morning I arrived at work and noticed Gail, our receptionist in the Trust offices, was not her cheerful self. I asked her if she was okay and she replied by telling me her husband Phil had just been admitted to our hospital having been diagnosed with leukaemia and his prognosis was terminal. Phil was a popular member of our Buildings and Works staff – everyone knew, respected and liked Phil. It was clearly devastating news.

In response I blurted out to Gail, 'I know a God who heals and can heal Phil – would you mind if I go and pray for him?' A nanosecond later my conscious brain caught up and I thought, 'What are you doing? You are the Chief Executive of the hospital and you have just offered to pray for God to heal a terminally ill man in the hospital who everyone knows. What if he's in a six-bed bay on the ward and nursing staff are watching? …' Just as my conscious brain shifted to over-drive, Gail said, 'That's really kind of you, but we are not religious people and I really don't think he would want that.'

Imagine my relief. I was off the hook! I went upstairs saying to the Lord, 'Well, I did offer, I can't force it on them, Lord.' (I'm just being honest – tell me you wouldn't think the same!)

The following day, when I came into work, I greeted Gail and she then said, 'You know you offered to pray for Phil? Well I spoke to him about it and he would really like that.' The Holy Spirit had well and truly got me on the hook after all!

My conscious thoughts were then no different to the previous day, but this time I had no excuse to wriggle out of my offer. So I arranged to go and see Phil on the ward.

Imagine my relief when the staff nurse told me he was in a single room and we would be alone. Again, I'm just being honest. I know, this was a dying man and here was I thinking about myself and my reputation.

Phil was really weak and barely able to talk. I prayed for his healing and the Lord gave me Psalm 23 to pray over him as he was truly walking 'through the valley of the shadow of death'. He seemed at peace when I left him.

A few days later Gail told me Phil had gone into remission and had been discharged home. Things were looking up.

Then after a few weeks of respite he was re-admitted to hospital as the leukaemia had progressed. My prayer for his healing didn't seem to have worked. But as soon as I knew, I arranged to visit him again on the ward. My PA rang the ward (yes – we had PAs in those days) and they said he was alone and it would be fine for me to visit him.

So this time I walked onto the ward and Phil was not in a single room but in an open six-bed bay. Not only that but he was not alone. He had three visitors. One of his visitors was the local councillor I had only ever spoken to across a crowded room in public meetings. And there was only one empty seat around Phil's bed – next to the local councillor (let's call him Gerald). So I sat down next to him and shook his hand and said how sorry I was about Phil's illness and that I hadn't realised they were friends. We sat and talked for a couple of minutes before I noticed there was complete silence around Phil's bed and Phil was sat up and grinning. I asked him why he was smiling and he said, 'I never dreamt I would see the day when you two spoke to each other!' I stayed a while longer and eventually took my leave, a bit frustrated that I hadn't been able to pray with Phil.

I got back to my office about an hour later and my PA had her phone in her hand, open-mouthed. She said, 'You'll never guess who wants to talk to you, but you won't want to talk to him, will you?' I said I didn't know unless she told me who it was. She told me it was Gerald and I said to put him through.

The first thing Gerald said to me was that the moment I sat down next to him, he was overcome by a feeling of holiness he had only ever experienced once in his life before, as a young boy in the presence of an Irish monk. In his own words he was describing the holy presence of God. I then listened to him tell me he felt he had not led a good life and he poured out his confession to me over the phone for forty-five minutes! I hardly said a word. I didn't need to. The Holy Spirit was doing it all.

The following day Gerald came to my office and shook my hand in front of my PA like a long-lost friend. She was thoroughly bemused!

Sadly, Phil died soon after. I attended his funeral with the Chairman of the Trust, and could not help but weep at the grace of God when the minister said that, at the request of Phil's widow, we were going to recite Psalm 23, which was his favourite.

Joel 2:32 says that those who call on the name of the Lord will be saved – so I knew that Phil, in calling on the Lord as his shepherd, may not have been healed, but he was saved.

And what of my relationship with Gerald?

Some months later we held a public consultation meeting over some significant changes we were proposing to our mental health services. After we had presented our case, Gerald stood up and took the floor in his customary way at public meetings. I could see my Chairman brace herself for the onslaught.

Basically the only thing he said was that he held both myself and my Chairman (who happened to be his political opponent) in the highest regard, and that anything we proposed was fine with him and he commended the meeting to support us! When he sat down my Chairman looked at me and mouthed silently the words, 'What just happened?'

And from that point on, for the next three years I stayed in the job, Gerald became my greatest public advocate.

In short, God had vindicated me publicly because I obeyed the prompting of the Holy Spirit to go and pray for a dying man. What a gracious God we serve!

Peace and assurance

After the two prophetic miracles, we entered 1997/98 knowing we had to seek God. As usual we had to plan our income and expenditure assuming a 3 per cent cash-efficiency saving, but that was now just a routine assumption for NHS financial planning.

You will have noted by now that the main focus of my prayers and the spiritual solutions has been about money, and for some that may serve to confirm (misleadingly) that all CEOs and FDs ever think about in healthcare is the financial bottom line. Internally within the Trust a lot of staff thought we were overly preoccupied with balancing the finances when it seemed that ours was one of the few Trusts that did so. The popular perception among staff was that lots of other Trusts got into deficit and then got bailed out financially. Even if it was true, there were three reasons to maintain our position:

- God would judge our leadership by His standards, not those of man, and the standard of integrity meant we had to manage with what we had and not spend what we didn't have. Business speaks of the 'Gold Standard'. I prefer the 'God Standard'.
- As a Trust we had a legal duty to break-even with our income and expenditure. If I believed that all authority was instituted by God (see chapter four) then I had to honour that authority and observe the law set by it. Back to the submission thing!
- At a practical level I preached 'Roger's law of economics' to our staff. This law meant that if we weren't in charge of our finances then someone else was. Whether in a business or domestic economy practically everyone can understand the ABC of economics that says if you spend more than you earn you get in debt, and if you're in debt someone else starts taking your decisions for you.

Just faith

After that diversion, let's get back to business. I had learned after the previous two years not to assume a particular spiritual solution (other than faith, of course) to our business issues. So this time I sought the Lord early on in the new financial year and didn't wait for a crisis. His answer was faith. Nothing more, nothing less. Just faith in Him.

In John 14:27 Jesus said to His disciples, 'Peace I leave with you, my peace I give you.' What ensued was probably the most peaceful year ever. There were no exceptional financial challenges at all that year and we just got on with the healthcare business. We got through the year in balance virtually all the way through and achieved some of the shortest waiting lists in the whole country. We were quoted by the Patients Association as amongst the best half-dozen hospitals in England for waiting-times in surgery and orthopaedics that year.

Although not as spectacular as the previous two years in terms of the spiritual solution, it was just as much a faith year as either of the previous ones. In fact I considered it to be God's best year for us precisely because there were no crises, just His peace. There was more a sense of ease, a sense of prosperity and achievement without striving or noise. It was peaceable and peaceful. Isn't that the way it should be if we're working in God's will? It was also the close of a distinct three-year period of spiritual solutions, a period in which my work life and approach moved beyond 'management solutions', albeit procured through prayer, into 'faith solutions' sought in prayer but which would make little management sense at all.

That's the beauty and excitement of faith solutions. They make no sense at all in terms of traditional management behaviour. Like David when pursued by Saul, or Joseph in jail, the spiritual solutions of the Bible are usually counter-intuitive. They take you outside of conventional management and business thinking into a realm of spiritual creativity and incredible blessing. But once you're in there, you have to make sure you stay there. And that's the theme for the next period.

So what?

So what lessons can we draw from these events, these miracles?

- The first has to be to submit the enterprise to God, with all its challenges and imperfections, and seek His answers to the issues.

- The second is to move in faith, despite the circumstances, when you know that you know you have His revelation by the Holy Spirit.

- Thirdly God judges our leadership by His standards, not those of man. Business speaks of the 'Gold Standard'. As believers we have to go for the 'God Standard'.

- If you are a leader, you are responsible for setting the spiritual atmosphere in the organisation. It doesn't have to be weird in the way you frame it and you can make aspects of it very practical. I give the example of preaching 'Roger's law of economics' to our staff, which meant that if we weren't in charge of our finances then someone else was.

Seven

A SALUTARY TALE

∞∞

In chapter four we talked about submission and obedience. Submission to the authorities and obedience to God.

So while the last chapter was a testimony to God's faithfulness when we are obedient, this chapter provides a cautionary tale about some spiritual truths I learned the hard way.

The trouble with patterns of history is you seldom see the big picture until the decisions have been made and it's too late to undo them.

Having enjoyed the ease and peace of 1997/98, the negotiating round in preparation for the following year was awful. A change of Government brought New Labour's declared intention to abolish the 'internal market' in the NHS and re-establish the primacy of Health Authorities over the disposition and pattern of health services. NHS Trusts had been largely autonomous to that point, albeit working within an overall Government policy framework.

For the NHS watchers among you, there is no doubt that the 'internal market' days of the NHS had created inequalities in service provision around the country and our approaches to managing diseases such as cancer and coronary heart disease lacked coherence nationally. Regardless of the political landscape, however, my role entailed leading the organisation to deliver the best possible healthcare to the local people. The change of political landscape may be explanatory, but it is not an attempt to excuse or justify my response to subsequent events.

While the previous year was peaceable and stable for us, the situation in most other Trusts around us was turbulent. Many had run up large overspends. The overview from the Health Authority seemed to be that our Trust had had it too easy. They made dramatic cuts to our contracts (we weren't the only ones) and required of us higher levels of efficiency than average. We felt we were being dealt with unjustly. Having brought down waiting times for virtually all specialties, the Health Authority decided only to purchase enough work to guarantee an eighteen-month maximum waiting time. Having balanced our books and delivered the efficiency targets for previous years we were now being asked to deliver higher levels of cash-releasing efficiency than Trusts that had failed to balance their books and who had longer waiting-times for patients waiting for surgery. We felt our record seemed to count for nothing and a sense of injustice rose within me. That was spiritual mistake number one.

Mistake number two happened after completion of the negotiating round when Chris and I were deliberating over our strategy for handling the year ahead. I said I thought it wouldn't do any harm if we ran a modest financial deficit so the Health Authority and the Regional Office of the Department of Health could see we had our problems too and that it wasn't the plain sailing they thought. We both thought our good record was being exploited, and so we agreed to aim to run to a modest deficit in the order of £250,000 a year. Not too big to be troublesome, but big enough to make a political point.

I might have got away with mistake number one if I had sought God to provide the answers. Instead I felt that what God had given us was being disrespected and, rather than being favoured and honoured, we were being persecuted. You will rightly tell me at this point that I should have remembered Jesus' words to His disciples about the world despising and persecuting those who follow Him (John 15:18-25). But I didn't. I not only failed to ask God what was happening but effectively I decided to reject His best for us. I was the one doing the dishonouring. The previous year had been a year of plain and simple faith, and here I was deciding I didn't want that godly peace and balance any more but had chosen instead to run a modest deficit. As I have said repeatedly, aligning yourself with God's will is a matter of the heart.

Unsurprisingly we got what we asked for. It was a modest deficit and it didn't create major turmoil. But it only took a month or so of the new financial year for me to know that I had been disobedient to God. I had rejected His best for us and I had lost the sense of peace He had given me in my leadership role. I shared my feelings with Chris and he agreed. We had to repent and seek God's forgiveness. We did so, but I knew there would be a price to that act of rejection and disobedience. We ended the year of 1997/98 with a deficit of £187,000, which was actually a lot better than it looked as if it was going to turn out. But I knew in my spirit that God had withdrawn His blessing. While I had repented and been forgiven, I had actually rejected God's blessing for that organisation, and as I was to discover it takes willing obedience and faith to restore the full blessing even after the forgiveness is given.

Let me interject something at this point about obedience. In chapter four we looked at authority and the spiritual principles about submission to authority. Remember Romans 13:1:

Everyone must submit himself to the governing authorities, for there is no authority except that which God has established.

Obedience to authority is a clear and simple way of determining whether one is submitted to the governing authorities. At one level, in this latest episode, I had rebelled against those in authority at the Health Authority and Department of Health Regional Office because I felt they were disrespecting what God had accomplished in the Trust. But my higher level of disobedience was towards God. In the book of Deuteronomy the Bible says:

The Lord will again delight in you and make you prosperous, just as he delighted in your fathers, if you obey the Lord your God and keep his commands ... and turn to the Lord your God with all your heart and with all your soul.

Deuteronomy 30:9-11

It wasn't that I chose to ignore or disobey what God told me to do in the circumstances we faced. It wasn't that I didn't pray. We had prayed. The mistake was that I didn't wait until I got the answer before deciding to run with a 'political' solution. I disobeyed firstly by not turning to God with all my heart and soul and pre-empting the answer He might have had for me. 1997/98 had been His best, but, in hindsight, I also became complacent and had started to take His blessing for granted. Presumption is an awful substitute for faith. Bad move, and not to be recommended.

Something I have learned over the years is that God is not a cosmic slot-machine into which you insert prayer and hope you hit the jackpot. Nor is He some kind of stockbroker who shifts your investments around until He finds the right one for your prosperity. The kind of spiritual 'dividends' I had enjoyed were the result of seeking God and having faith in His answers. Faith is 'being sure of what of we hope for and certain of what we do not see' (Hebrews 11:1). None of it could have happened without faith. So please don't get any smart ideas about using the principles I describe in this book in any way cynically. I fear the results would then be worse than if you hadn't used them at all. Galatians 6:7 says, 'God cannot be mocked. A man reaps what he sows.' The faith journey in business can be exhilarating, but it can also be disastrous if the motives and goals are wrong, or if one attempts to manipulate the Word of God cynically for personal gain.

I made the point earlier that it takes more than just repentance for the full blessing to be restored. While I knew God had forgiven me for the decision to run a deficit it also became apparent that the special answers to our situation had started to dry up. We had wanted to show the authorities that we had our problems like everyone else, and sure enough that's what we now got.

The 'modest' deficit of £187,000 became a larger one in the following year, and in my final year with the Trust (2000/01) it became a really problematic year-end deficit of £860,000.

During that year the pressure for the Trust to dissolve and merge also became irresistible. I do not attribute the merger to that act of disobedience, because the merger made sense from a long-term service standpoint, and was the natural result of a well-developed strategic alliance with a larger neighbouring Trust. It was certainly the case, however, that the Trust's corporate strength and bargaining power in the merger were compromised by its financial weakness.

Obedience to the rescue

Tying spiritual weights around your feet is not a good idea when you're trying to swim. My disobedience in 1998 had been the spiritual weights that pulled us down. Part of the problem, of course, is knowing whether you've still got them on. And that's part of the challenge with spiritual stuff. It's easier to see the material, physical evidence of success or failure, whereas in spiritual matters that same evidence is only a pointer to something less tangible. Equally the connections are not always obvious until the spiritual lights get turned on.

The background to this part of the chapter is rooted in the struggle of the later years described in the previous section. Throughout those years there was a move on the part of the Health Authority and Regional Office to dissolve the Trust and merge its acute hospital services, in particular, with the a larger neighbouring Trust. At the same time I had become aware that the higher echelons in the NHS thought I should move on to a 'bigger' job. Most particularly I kept hearing quiet suggestions that I should move to a larger acute Hospitals Trust job, where the relationship between the Health Authority and the Trust was known to be problematic, and apparently they saw me as the guy to fix it.

My ambitions, however, lay elsewhere. The Trust they wanted me to lead was carrying one of the largest financial debts (£4.1m) in the country in proportion to its turnover. I knew from the outside looking in that its management's relationships with the rest of the NHS in the area were not good. I knew from living in the area that the hospital services themselves were good and had a good reputation. But the management challenges I also knew to be enormous. To cut a long story short, when the CEO job became vacant I didn't want it and didn't apply. The fact it was advertised at a salary about 15 per cent less than I was earning didn't help either! So I ignored the quiet suggestions and instead put my hat in the ring to take the local Health Authority CEO job which had also fallen vacant. In fact both posts were advertised at the same time, and in my mind the choice was absolutely clear. I say 'in my mind' deliberately, as it would be wrong to say I had prayed it through and sought God about the choice. I just assumed He would naturally agree with me!

Discussions with a whole range of key people encouraged me to proceed with the Health Authority job, and I got to the final interview, but I didn't get the job. I was devastated. I had been praying for months about my future and I had thought God had lined it all up for me to step into the top job in the area health system. But no. God clearly had other plans. As if to emphasise the point, the job I failed to get was abolished by a Government re-organisation of Health Authorities only six months after the new CEO took up post.

Just a few weeks after the interview for the Health Authority post, I went with my family to our annual church Faith Camp. In the meantime the NHS Trust CEO job had not been filled and remained vacant. I was adamant, however, that I wasn't interested and, therefore, the re-advertisement was irrelevant. It became very relevant, however, when God got my attention in the middle of a meeting at Faith Camp, where an American speaker (yes, another American! – what is it about these guys?) by the name of Bishop Harry Jackson was speaking about our relevance as believers in the communities in which we live, and

I was hit with an unequivocally clear call from God to apply. Everything within me screamed 'No!' I tried to reason that God wouldn't tell me to go for a job that meant a 15 per cent drop in salary (just being honest!) and a big financial and relationship mess to sort out again. But I couldn't get out of it. I just could not ignore what God was telling me.

I know some of you will find this a bit difficult and will justifiably ask how I knew. Did I hear an audible voice or what was it? I can only say that, as a believer, you know when God is instructing you in something by the feeling in your spirit. And this was something in human terms that I had absolutely no desire to do. But until I made the decision that I would apply, the Holy Spirit simply would not get off my case. God's direction to me left me in turmoil. My agreement to pursue the command, to obey, was the thing that gave me peace. As soon as I submitted to His direction, and resolved to go for the job, my sense of peace returned. I know it sounds like there is major potential for self-delusion here, but the best way I can describe the feeling is that moment when you put right the thing that has been nagging your conscience and suddenly you know you've done the right thing and have peace of mind. And you wish you'd done it earlier and saved yourself the grief of all that guilt!

The first thing I did to make sure I couldn't wriggle off the hook was to tell my wife Vicky what God had told me to do. If I'd told no-one I would have kept wriggling and reasoning. But telling Vicky meant I now had no escape, because even if I had wanted to, I knew she wouldn't let me. So the commitment was made. I had decided to obey.

The process of applying was not straightforward. It was handled by 'head hunters'. I decided to handle the salary issue up front and transparently pre-interview. I was given to understand my current salary would be matched, only to have the position change a couple of days prior to interview allegedly by the Trust Chairman's veto, leaving me feeling the recruiters had not been honest with me and the Chairman didn't want me.

While I had managed to close some of the salary gap, it would still mean a 10 per cent drop and the loss of other benefits such as a lease car. The only thing that kept me committed was knowing that I was being obedient to God's command. From a human standpoint I wanted to withdraw from the process almost every day. Being a 'local' candidate, and living locally, were more a hindrance than a benefit because people naturally thought I just wanted a job close to home. I also assumed they thought I was running away from the merger in my current job, but of course they were all too polite to say so. I had to work very hard to convince people like my prospective Chairman that I genuinely wanted the job when the real reason for my application probably would have had the short-listing panel assigning it to the waste-paper bin.

I'm waffling. Let's cut to the chase. You guessed by now that I got the job. On the one hand my heart was breaking on having to leave my current Trust at the height of its difficulties. On the other hand I knew I was doing what God wanted. And one thing I have learned is that God never asks us to do something that doesn't have a purpose.

At a material level I was leaving a Trust with a yearly turnover of £55 million and 2,000 staff for one with a turnover of £84 million and 3,200 staff. I was moving from a pretty low profile 'quiet' Trust with a good reputation (quiet because it was never really a problem to higher authority in the NHS) to one with a high profile and regarded as a problem to be sorted out. And I was taking a 10 per cent salary cut and accepting a package without any of the benefits I had enjoyed for the previous eight years. Don't get me wrong, I was still going to be paid very well. But relatively speaking I was taking a big drop in earnings and benefits to do what appeared to be a much harder job.

What happened?

The Bible says you test the quality of the tree by its fruit. I was there for three and a half years.

There were none of the spectacular tithing or prophetic financial miracles you read about in the last chapter, but the turn-around in the fortunes of the Trust was equally miraculous. To focus again on the financial results (because you can check them from the audited accounts) the results changed from the £4.1 million debt of 1999/2000, to break-even (no deficit at all) in the following three years. That might seem laudable but quite ordinary unless you understand the context of the immense financial pressures on hospitals in the south-east of England, whereby my Trust was the only one of eight acute Hospital Trusts in the region to meet its financial targets in three consecutive years without borrowing or external financial support. I know full well my colleague Chief Executives and their respective Trust Boards in the other hospitals in the area neither wanted nor welcomed their financial plight. In that context our results were simply outstanding.

During that two-year period the Trust's income grew by about 35 per cent, and our reputation within the overall health community was transformed. Of course we had our detractors. Who doesn't? And of course there will be plenty of people who will look at our circumstances and find a rational explanation. But they would miss the point completely and utterly. Disagree with me if you wish, but I know in my heart that the root of the Trust's recovery lay in my obedience to God's command to go and do the job there. And He was the one who did it all, not me.

In Deuteronomy 11:13-15 it says:

So if you faithfully obey the commands I am giving you today – to love the LORD your God and to serve him with all your heart and with all your soul – then I will send rain on your land in its season, both autumn and spring rains, so that you may gather in your grain, new wine and oil. I will provide grass in the fields for your cattle, and you will eat and be satisfied.

The biblical promise is that if we obey His commands, God will provide the resources in season to prosper our work. I had been obedient to His command to take a job I didn't want, and I had worked conscientiously with my new team and other local colleagues to get the Trust's working relationships and finances back in good order. But we still had a major black cloud hanging over the Trust, which was the cumulative debt of £6.8 million built up during the two-year period before my tenure. So while we were hitting our annual financial targets to break-even, we were still not making any in-roads on the underlying debt. Then early in 2004, and before our accounts were closed for the previous year, we received a grant of £6.5 million to clear the cumulative debt. In many ways I found this the most awesome and humbling of God's gifts. The accountants can explain away the technical rationale and will put this down to the system rewarding good financial stewardship, and at a material level they would be right. Nor do I wish in any way to diminish the professionalism and effort of the management team that worked hard for the results. I also know I risk professional ridicule by attributing the results to my spiritual obedience, as the organisational leader, to God. But I simply cannot describe this turn-round and restoration of the Trust's financial fortunes in any other way.

Psalm 5:12 says, 'For surely, O LORD, you bless the righteous: you surround them with your favour as with a shield.' I believe that is precisely what the Lord did in that situation, wiping away our debt by His grace. Just as Jesus did with our sins on the cross.

I am not claiming here some messianic mission from God. What I want you to understand is that God is genuinely interested in your fortunes at work. He's interested in seeing His kingdom principles make a difference in the work you do. On earth as it is in heaven.

He emblazoned the principles of righteousness and integrity on my heart and my approach to my work some fifteen years earlier. And here I was in 2004 experiencing the rewards 'in season'.

The favour of God

God is interested in our personal welfare and fortunes too. At a personal level, my change of job took me into what turned out to be one of only six out of twenty-six CEO jobs in the NHS in the region that survived the major organisational changes introduced by Government in April 2002. What I had regarded as a potential poisoned chalice was actually one of the few islands of stability in the whole region.

In addition, during that first year in the new job I had another encounter with God in a most unexpected but delightful way.

To give you some context for this next little miracle I should explain that in 1997 my wife and I had opened our own charitable trust to ensure our tithing and giving was done in the most tax-efficient way. Every year I had reclaimed tax relief back for the charitable trust and invested it back into the Giving Fund.

Then one Sunday evening, as we were in the middle of worship at church, a little voice in my head told me I had a personal income tax rebate due for the period 1997–2000. Now please be assured that I don't spend my time at church thinking about money and tax rebates when I should be listening to the preacher or worshipping God. I was actually deep and lost in worship, and wondered where on earth this thought had come from. I did the good 'Christian' thing and rebuked the devil for trying to divert me from worshipping God. But the voice persisted. Once again it wasn't a booming voice or an angelic apparition; it was just a quiet little thought that was totally and utterly out of place with what I was doing. What I heard was that while I had reclaimed the tax rebate for the charitable trust for those three years, I could also claim it personally for myself. Now I admit to being no great expert on tax law in relation to charities, but I had reasoned way back in 1998, when completing the first annual return for the charity, that I could only reclaim a rebate for the charity and not for myself. Or so I thought.

Well I must admit I struggled with this thought in my head, but I thought I'd take a bit of biblical advice and 'test the spirits' (1 John 4:1 says clearly, 'Dear friends, do not believe every spirit, but test the spirits to see whether they are from God …'). So I prayed and said to the Lord quite honestly that I thought what I'd heard was not lawful. And the Holy Spirit replied to me that I should ask the Inland Revenue. Well I thought that was a pretty practical piece of advice. After all I didn't want to claim something that was not lawfully mine, and it couldn't do any harm to ask as long as I told the full truth. If it was just my imagination and not the Holy Spirit after all, then all I'd lose was the time spent enquiring. And it was only after I settled on that course of action that I had peace enough to return to the worship.

So I wrote to the Inland Revenue the following day and laid my cards on the table about having claimed the rebate for the Giving Fund during those three years, and they wrote back to me asking for facts and figures, which I then supplied. They then responded and told me I *was* due a rebate for the three years in question. And the most incredible thing was that the rebate was almost exactly the amount of net pay I had lost that year in taking the new job at the reduced salary. How cool was that!

The whole episode was for me such a delightful expression of God's character and His interest in my welfare. The Lord had supplied more than enough finances for me and my family and I hadn't been praying about money issues. I hadn't been complaining to God that He'd got me to do a more pressured job for less pay. And that evening, as I was deep in worship, nothing could have been further from my mind than money or tax rebates. I remember being wrapped up in worshipping my God, and then suddenly this thought comes out of nowhere telling me I'm due a tax rebate! But that is exactly when God communicates most clearly with us, when we press into His presence and forget our cares and issues, when we forget about us, and focus instead on His majesty and awesome power. It was His free gift, His reward for my obedience.

When the time then came for my salary review in mid-2002, the original salary gap, having been filled by God's gift to me the previous year, was more than made good by the Trust Board's Remuneration Committee, and was considerably beyond my expectation. When my Chairman told me of their decision I struggled not to shed a tear of gratitude for God's faithfulness to me. But it was again a sign of confirmation that the Lord had been pleased with my obedience. It wasn't about the money – I had more than enough – it was about His loving faithfulness.

Anointing is personal

After three years in the job a new set of Government reforms were introduced to develop NHS Foundation Trusts, and a review of acute hospitals in the area was announced. I had now been a Chief Executive for over eleven years, which was long enough for me to think the latest batch of Government reforms to be 'smoke and mirrors' (cynical I know!). The hospitals review would be the third time we had gone around this particular mulberry bush in my time, and I could anticipate the pain of the process and the public anguish it would generate were unlikely to render anything of genuine value. I was truly thankful for the time I had spent in the NHS, but also recognising I was becoming unable to dance to the political tunes any longer with genuine conviction and belief. And if I couldn't apply myself with all my heart to my work, then it was time for a change. I recognised the risk of drifting into an experienced but politically cynical dance that was unlikely to sit well with my ethics and integrity.

I started to seek God about my future all over again. He began to revive my spirit and dreams through a book from a friend for my fiftieth birthday called *Wild at Heart* by John Eldredge. Those of you familiar with the book will know it's all about God's design for the heart of a man. In reading it I realised I had lost my sense of adventure and battle to fight. At the same time my daughters were feeding me on a musical diet of Switchfoot on our car journeys and, when I finally got beyond the guitar riffs and rock rhythms and listened to the lyrics, I found God speaking to me through their classic tracks 'Meant to Live' and 'Dare to Move'. The combination of Eldredge and Switchfoot proved irresistible for my spirit. I had to find a new battle to fight, a new adventure to pursue, and I needed to move!

Surprising as it may sound, turning NHS Trusts into financially sustainable organisations was not a great motivator for me. What really sparked me was opening people's eyes to new possibilities, seeing beyond their apparent limitations, helping people transform and go beyond themselves. I had found myself working at my best as a CEO (or at least working at its most enjoyable) when I was in a facilitative and inspirational mode, enabling people to be the best they could be, and so I set my sights on consultancy as my chosen adventure.

Around the same time (funny that!) and out of the blue I found myself invited to go and join a Christian charity and ministry as CEO. I had been a Trustee for several years, so we were well known to each other, but I was both humbled and flattered to be considered for the role.

I also thought my job was done at my Hospitals Trust. The fortunes and reputation of the Trust had turned around, the financial slate was wiped clean and I thought I was leaving it in good order for the future. I knew the new battles weren't mine to fight.

So I decided it was time to leave the NHS after twenty-six years and pursue a new adventure in the consultancy business. I figured the charity neither needed a full time CEO, and nor could it afford one. So I took the role on a part-time basis, a couple of days a week, and developed my consulting business in parallel.

And that's where I learned that God's anointing is personal. This is no matter for boasting and I watched the situation as an outsider with deep regret, but in just over a year the Hospitals Trust was back in deep financial trouble, significantly worse even than the position I had inherited, and from which it never really recovered until it went into a merger with a neighbouring Trust some four years later.

Would it have been different if I had stayed? Only God knows. But He also knew my heart wasn't in it, so in late 2004 He moved me on to my new adventure.

So what?

What lessons did I draw from this period?

- I learned how easy it is to fall into complacency in the blessings of

God. We went from the peaceful mountain-top to the shadowy and troublesome valley in three years, because I had grieved the Holy Spirit by rejecting His best for the organisation I led and I had not upheld His standard of integrity. We have to stay alert in the Spirit at all times.

- If we truly repent of spiritual misdemeanours in our work and business God can restore the anointing we have lost. He did it for King David after his adultery with Bathsheba and killing of her husband. And He can do it for us, too, if we truly repent and turn back to Him.

- The key to restoring the anointing to lead, albeit in a different organisation, was through obedience to His direction to apply for a job I didn't want and battle through and overcome all the conflicts in my mind.

- The Holy Spirit can speak to us in the most unlikely of situations if we will only take notice and follow His Word to test the spirits.

- The anointing from God is on the believer and the spiritual environment they establish. Unless the organisation is consecrated to God by its continuing leadership, the anointing will leave with the believer.

Eight

A BATTLE TO FIGHT, AN ADVENTURE TO PURSUE

∞∞

When you have spent your working life in paid employment, living on a guaranteed monthly salary, the move to the fee-earning world of consulting and part-time employment in the charitable sector was scary and required a big step of faith. My children were savvy enough to recognise the risk to their lifestyle, so the change was not free of internal family challenge! Welcome to the real world, I hear so many of you say.

Those of you who have made the move to set up your own business will know the only thing that beats the joy of getting your first paying client is getting your first invoice paid. Banking that cheque was the moment I felt I was really in business!

The period from 2005 to 2008 was another one of deep learning, not only about the realities, technicalities and demands of business life, but also about learning how it was *not* to be 'in charge' for the first time in twelve years. I had always been realistic enough to know that I would not be a spiritual leader of the Ministry regardless of my job title, but I also had to get used to the idea that consultancy clients don't necessarily follow the advice they pay you to give!

God was faithful in providing for my family in this new phase of my working life, and the consultancy was ticking along nicely. But in the Ministry I found myself doing exactly the stuff I had done in my early CEO days of the NHS, having to cut the employed staff dramatically twice within three years to live within the organisation's financial means and keep the bank from the door. It was necessary for the charity's continued existence, but it was not what I thought I had signed up to do. It certainly didn't feel like I was opening people's eyes to new possibilities.

Then from mid-2007 I started to feel like I was wandering in a working and spiritual desert. I was now working two days a week for the Ministry on a consulting basis but outside of that work promises were being broken by prospective clients, and my consulting work had effectively dried up. By the autumn my heart was sinking at the prospect of a second round of major job cuts as the charity's financial position continued to head south.

In December of that year I was in a management meeting with two of the three elders to finalise the plans for financial restructuring. They had fully reassured me that they wanted me to stay on in my current capacity when I had another of my 'what on earth have I just said?' moments and found myself blurting out that I thought I should give up the CEO role and cut back to a day a week in a business management role.

So I had not only just offered to step down from being the CEO, I had also just offered to cut my consulting income in half!

Once said, of course, it could not be unsaid. And, based on previous experience, I knew the Lord was in it because I had complete peace.

On the morning of Monday 7 January 2008, the first working day after a long Christmas and New Year break, I found myself preparing to meet the Ministry founder and eldership to advise them formally of my stepping down from the CEO role and my proposal to go to a day a week to provide business and governance support to the charity. I still had no other consulting work. But I believed the Holy Spirit had prompted my unplanned blurt a couple of weeks earlier, so I took the step of faith.

And then the miracles started again!

As I was about to leave home for my meeting with the eldership I got a text from a director of a company called Tricordant, Alastair Mitchell-Baker. I had rung Alastair a few months earlier on a lead from a colleague in the consulting business. I had checked out the Tricordant website, of course, before my call, and found myself fascinated by their Celtic logo and consulting model they called the Tricord. As soon as I introduced myself Alastair had said, 'Are you the Roger Greene who was the Christian Chief Executive in the NHS?' It quickly became apparent that while we had never met, we had common acquaintances in the NHS when Alastair had worked there. Most amazing of all, the Tricordant logo was a Celtic symbol for the Trinity, and the consulting model was based on the divine interplay between the Father, Son and Holy Spirit. Our conversation flowed quickly as it emerged that Tricordant were a company of Christians operating in the commercial market.

We subsequently met, but there were no immediate opportunities to work together.

Anyway, to get back to 7 January. In the text Alastair asked if I would be interested in being a part of an urgent bid he had been invited to put together by a high-profile national client on behalf of a Government minister. I naturally said yes – and then went about my business of resigning my CEO position.

Later that afternoon Alastair was back in touch to say the bid was successful and could I start straight away. He was as astounded as I was that the client approved the bid so quickly for a team of four of us to work for them without any interview, CVs or written submission. It turned out to be the highest earning single contract of my consulting career up to that point and took me into a quality of client assignment and places at national level that I could never have won alone.

It was a clear statement for me of God's faithfulness and favour that He should release that opportunity only hours after I took my step of faith to voluntarily halve my consulting income.

And so began the next step of my career journey with God, and a regular flow of new, interesting and well-paid work in 2008 as an associate to Tricordant.

It wasn't long before the two directors of Tricordant asked me to pray about joining them, and they committed to do the same. This was clearly not a company who simply followed the normal rules, but brought God into the recruitment equation, including a discerning process with the company's Advisory Council, a group of experienced and wise Christians who all had significant career histories of their own.

Tricordant mission and story

Tricordant was founded in 2005 by Irwin Bidgood, Simon Thane and Alastair Mitchell-Baker in the UK. A twin venture was set up in New Zealand by Tim Pidsley and Les Rudd, based on the same consulting model and with the same mission.

The founding mission of the company is Isaiah 61:1, 'to proclaim freedom for the captives and release from darkness for the prisoners', all in the context of the workplace and the design and development of work.

The focus of Tricordant is to help transform workplaces, making them whole, healthy, productive and enjoyable places to work. The founders recognised that many workplaces had become inhumane production lines, where work was repetitive and dispiriting, lacking any sense of deeper purpose for people. You only have to look at the proliferation of modern-day call centres to see the continuing pattern of detached rules-driven work where employees feel remote and detached from the principal purposes of their business, and risk real separation from their clients.

Irwin, Alastair and Simon created Tricordant to be a catalyst to enable organisations to transform themselves from within and fulfil their purpose and potential, so that their business, employees and communities could be freed to be fruitful, with meaningful jobs in a whole and healthy environment. The consulting practice is based on a healthy mix of biblical theology about work and evidence-based practice.

Given their mission and my story, how could this not work?

Irwin, Simon and Alastair had worked together as associates of Christian Schumacher, author of *God in Work*, and they built on Christian's work in their search for a divine pattern to the organisation and development of work. Irwin's spiritual and intellectual curiosity had been a real driving force in the formation and development of the new company, but sadly he died with the company only two years old. While I never got to meet him, I have been grateful to know his widow Rosalie, who has continued to carry the flame for the Bidgood family in the work of the company through the Advisory Council.

Christian Commercial Fellowship

In January 2009 I bought the shareholding I was offered and became a co-owner and director.

In Tricordant we aim to be a Kingdom business, to model an approach to business that would be pleasing to the Lord. We don't always get it right, but that's because we are human, and we live and work in a human system.

We don't claim to have it all sorted, but it may help those of you in business to share some practical ways in which we try to express our identity.

Legally we are a private limited company. We describe ourselves, however, as a Christian commercial fellowship. Each of the three words is important in our understanding of what it means to us to be a Kingdom business.

Christian

By Christian we mean the business is owned by believers. Shared faith has to be a 'line in the sand' for the ownership and direction of a company that bases its consulting model on the Holy Trinity. Our employed team, however, is made up of believers and non-believers. We also have a network of Partner Consultants with whom we co-work regularly, and again they are a healthy mix of Christians and non-Christians, but who all respect and appreciate our values. In respect of employment and partnership the foundations of our relationship are shared ethics and mission. It's all a matter of the heart.

We are a geographically dispersed company, each working from offices at home, with Nottinghamshire, Brighton and the Brecon Beacons the current extremes of our geography. We congregate around the Reading area when we hold our monthly team meetings. It means we don't have the water-cooler or office corridor moments of more traditional office-based consultancies, so we have to operate with different disciplines.

As an exclusively Christian organisation when I joined in 2009 it was relatively easy to operate in a dynamic of faith and prayer in our team and business meetings. As the employed team and network of partners has grown we have had to work hard to find ways to exercise our faith while accommodating and respecting the beliefs of non-Christians without them feeling excluded. Our practice now is to open our monthly team meetings with a voluntary half hour of scheduled prayer and also close with a voluntary time of prayer for those wishing to stay behind after the business agenda is completed. Team members and partners who are not Christians respect the fact that we do no compromise or water-down our faith, but we don't force them to participate either. Faith is a voluntary thing. We also open and close the business parts of our team meetings with brief prayer so the items on the agenda are spiritually covered. We have prayer-Skypes pretty well every week (but the discipline is hard for everyone to join with busy schedules) and when Christian team members are working together on a client project they will usually pray briefly before workshops or client meetings.

The truth be told, outside of our monthly meetings, it's difficult to build hard and fast disciplines that will involve everyone in prayer because our work requires team members to be directly engaged with clients around the country or travelling. We are constantly seeking to get this right and are far from perfect. We have a single-page Tricordant Rule to govern our fellowship and a declaration of faith that recognises the Lord as our Managing Director. We run a closed social network on WhatsApp that allows us to pray for and encourage one another at any time. One of our team members has responsibility to be mindful of our spiritual health and ensure we have regular prayer. So we have a number of building blocks and disciplines in place to keep us right before the Lord. And of course there is the onus on each and every individual to pray and participate in the corporate prayer as well as their own prayer life. It never feels like it's enough, but the Lord knows our hearts.

We have an annual retreat over three days to pray together and spend time seeking the Lord for the business. I will say more about our retreats shortly.

Commercial

We operate in a commercial market, serving clients across all sectors of commerce, public service and the third sector.

It's important to say that we aim to operate with both faith and commercial discipline, not just with one or the other. The Lord is our provider, but He also expects us to use the gifts and skills He has given us and not simply to wait for Him to give us the next client. I will come shortly to a key prophetic word He gave the company in 2010, which is based on the disciples exercising their skills and knowledge as fishermen.

To work as fishermen the disciples needed to tend their boats, keep them seaworthy, maintain their nets, and work as teams. And when they caught their miraculous catches, as guided by Jesus in Luke 5 and John 21, they also had to land them and prepare the fish for market. And when the catches were too big to land alone, they had associates to call on for help. They doubtless had plenty of heavy lifting to accompany the joy and wonder of the catch.

Being commercial is not just about being financially savvy and sharp. We absolutely have to know our 'value' to the market and price our work competitively. We have to be clear about the boundaries of client assignments and have disciplines in place to monitor how contracts are performing, and re-negotiate when the client changes the brief or we believe a change of brief is required. We regard ourselves as accountable to the client for the resources they have committed with us. We aim to 'love our client' and there are times when we go the extra mile to support them in achieving their aims but also times when we draw a clear line if we think the client is going down the wrong path. In the end it's all about relationship.

Being commercial also means we have to be disciplined about our ways of working, both with clients and in our internal operations. It means having sales and marketing pipelines as well as faith. It means competing for tenders as well as seeking God for new relationships and contract extensions. It means cultivating and maintaining networks of relationships as well as good prayer disciplines. It means having good data protection policies as well as words of prophecy.

I want to sound a cautionary note here for Christian business and organisational leaders. Being a Christian is not necessarily sufficient to be part of a company or Christian business. From wider experience I have seen business owners make poor recruitment decisions based simply on someone's faith. Having the right skills and attitude to client service must accompany faith in this regard. It is a sad truth that a non-Christian with the right skills and client-serving values will usually do better work than a Christian who lacks both the skills to do the work and the understanding of a client's aims and objectives.

From the standpoint of the Christian seeking to join a company or enterprise, the other side of the coin is that your profession of faith alone is insufficient qualification. Do not expect a Christian leader or business-owner to employ you solely on grounds of your faith. Your faith gives you a wonderful advantage to succeed, but remember it must be through the expression of Kingdom work values such as gifting, diligence and 'working as for the Lord and not for men' (Colossians 3:23).

You will keep hearing me say the rubber hits the road when it comes to money. And even in the most spiritually refined Kingdom business there has to be a fair and equitable reward structure. As Tricordant has grown, we now have directors (the business owners) and employed staff. Our reward system for directors is a basic salary plus dividends based on equal share-holding per full-time director, and for employed staff it is a salary plus bonus arrangement in line with their levels of responsibility. The staff bonus tracks director dividends as a percentage, so everyone in the company has a direct interest in the profitability of the company.

While we want everyone to have a material interest in the commercial success of the company, we see ourselves as a fellowship, and have purposely chosen to avoid a reward system based on personal performance. As any commercial consultancy would do, we track individual utilisation rates and sales, but we do so for openness, accountability and personal development planning, and not to inform reward.

Fellowship

Tricordant was founded with the aim of being a fellowship of equals. We know the very word 'equality' is loaded with meaning socially and economically, but at its most fundamental we mean equal in the eyes of God. It means inclusion, mutual respect, empowerment, trust and voice for all – but it does not mean democracy where everyone gets to vote on everything, and directors have responsibility before God to exercise leadership where decisions are required.

We believe a distinguishing feature of a Kingdom business should be in the quality of relationship among us, and I hope the illustration I am about to give will serve to make the point well.

In 2008 the directors convened the first spiritual retreat for the company. The intention was to spend three days together in prayer, seeking God for the company. While there were half a dozen of us gathered in a retreat centre in Somerset, Tim Pidsley joined us from New Zealand by Skype to make it a truly global occasion! It soon became clear it was a strategic time for the company and has since become part of our company's annual rhythm and ritual.

A retreat never passes without some significant prophecy or revelation of God's will for us, and the autumn 2009 retreat was especially important and prophetic. The Lord spoke to us through John 15:12:

> *My command is this: Love each other as I have loved you.*

The Lord was not showing us where to find our work or which markets to develop. He was telling us *how to be* with one another.

As a company we had been prospering financially and had no idea at the time of the peaks and troughs to follow, whether in matters of health, commercial work, pipeline drought or even the kind of relational tensions that can spring up in any business or workplace. We are broken human vessels, and sometimes behave as such, but the clear word of the Lord to love one another has been the anchor that has kept us grounded and bound to one another regardless of the circumstances.

We don't always agree with one another and, as with any human organisation, we have our fall-outs. The call to love one another in fellowship, however, over-rules everything.

Power of prayer

In March 2009 Alastair and I were invited to interview for a major health and social care contract to redevelop services for the elderly in an area in the east of England. It was a highly contested shortlist, with a downside that the interviews were not only being conducted by a panel of ten people from a variety of different organisations, but were being held in a Masonic hall. The added downside was that neither Alastair nor I had any track record in health and local government partnership strategy development for the elderly.

We were invited to wait in the ante-room to the Masonic chapel. We both felt a sense of spiritual oppression in the place, so rather than spend our waiting time rehearsing for the interview, we spent it praying, binding and loosing in good biblical fashion.

Then came our turn for the interview. We both found ourselves going off script in our presentation and getting a bit carried away. And then in the plenary Q&A a most remarkable thing happened – out of nowhere a member of the panel said how she had felt completely overwhelmed by the passion in our presentation, and then another member of the panel (the Finance representative, no less) chipped in and said, 'You know, I felt overwhelmed too!' Clearly the Holy Spirit had moved the panel in our favour and it will come as no surprise that we won the bid and started an assignment that subsequently triggered seven years of continuous work with the health commissioners and local authorities in the region.

Being thankful

We aspire to be a Kingdom business, but we also operate in the realities of the market.

In 2010 the UK was going through the hardest sustained economic recession any of us could remember in our lifetimes. Job losses, pay freezes and cuts in working hours were a common experience for believers and non-believers alike. Trading conditions in business were really difficult in all sectors of the economy.

We work in a consultancy market that depends on discretionary spend by clients and we only earn if we have client orders. Small- and medium-size businesses like ours were going to the wall because the work had simply dried up. Even the larger consulting companies were typically reducing staff by up to 50 per cent.

Our story, though, was different. While we use the kind of sales and marketing techniques used by most businesses of our size, we also pray together and believe for God to supply the client work. We thanked God that we had sustained our turnover over the previous three years, which anyone in our business would tell you at the time was a minor miracle in itself. But my next story is about a specific miracle the Lord did for us back at the beginning of 2010.

Like any business we monitor our 'pipeline' of proposals and potential client work to be able to forecast cash flow and continuing profitability. In February 2010, however, our pipeline was drying up. We had some current projects drawing to a close, but after that there were few active prospects.

I personally had gone a month without substantive client work and was hanging on a call from a client who had suggested there might be follow-up work to a project we had just completed. Then he emailed me on a Friday evening to say he was sorry but they no longer needed our support.

The following Monday morning, in my prayer time, I was reading how Israel went out to war led by worshippers praising God for the splendour of His holiness (2 Chronicles 20). It reminded me of a prophetic word to my church from our senior pastor, from Isaiah 54:1.

Sing, O barren woman, you who never bore a child; burst into song, shout for joy, you who were never in labour; because more are the children of the desolate woman than of her who has a husband.

The command was to rejoice and praise God in the middle of the barrenness. Now you might not associate Isaiah 54 with the business world, but the witness in my spirit was so strong that I got up and sang to the Lord over the barrenness of the company pipeline. I was moved to act physically as well as spiritually to activate the promise of God in the scripture.

Within ten days we had received three new contracts for work! The client who said on the previous Friday they didn't need us emailed me to say they were mistaken and could we please continue to support them after all. The other two contracts were out of the blue from previous clients without any prior notice.

In 1 Thessalonians 5:18 Paul exhorts us to 'give thanks in all circumstances, for this is God's will for you in Christ Jesus'. A dry business pipeline might not seem the most promising of business circumstances, but the spiritual key to our business issue was our thankfulness and worship.

Gone fishing

You should have the picture by now that work and business are seldom plain sailing. On the other hand it wouldn't be a walk of faith if there were never any obstacles to overcome.

Like any business we can only pay our salaries and bills if the client work is coming in. In June 2011, however, our pipeline was drying up again. We were coming to the end of one major project and had a couple of other small projects on the go – but again had no active proposals, tenders or invitations to bid for work. Our profits for the first two quarters of the year were the lowest we had ever experienced. The circumstances were not looking good.

And then in the summer of 2011 the Lord did something quite extraordinary.

The previous summer the Lord had given us a prophetic word from John 21 to 'throw our nets on the right side of the boat' – remember how Jesus instructed the disciples at the end of a long and fruitless night-shift fishing on the Sea of Galilee? We were blessed by some good work that summer and autumn but it never felt as though our nets were full or the prophetic word had been accomplished. This time, however, in the summer of 2011, we believed that prophetic word was now in season for us and we prayed and believed the Lord that He was going to fill our nets.

Within two weeks my colleague directors received three unsolicited approaches for major proposals from prospective clients in industry, health and social care, and international development. Two of the three approaches meant we had to compete with 'the big boys' of the consulting world to win the work – and when we prayed as a team the Lord spoke to two of us at the same time that He was pitting us as David against the Goliaths of the business. If you are not big on prophetic words you might think we were maybe getting a bit fanciful and deluded to comfort ourselves – except that we won each of the contracts – and in one of them the Goliath was given three shots at winning to see if they could match us. One of the contracts turned out to be three-times bigger than anything we had ever won in the six-year history of the company and another was our third largest contract ever.

But it didn't stop there. I received an invitation to bid for work at very short notice for a contract we had missed when it was advertised – again we won the contract. Then at a Church Life Group meeting, when we were praying in small groups one of my friends said he saw a fish circling our boat with an open mouth. Two days later I was approached by the 'short notice' client who asked if we would be willing to double the contract we had just begun that very day. That same client then recommended us to another for a similar contract which we were also subsequently awarded.

Around the same time one of my director colleagues was approached by an international development organisation we had never heard of in the Far East. He put together a proposal only to be told that the contract had already been given to us before the proposal was submitted. Believe it or not, the agency's mission was about the development of indigenous fish stocks in the Third World!

To cut a long story short, after the first six months of the year when turnover and profits were really low, the second six months were so extraordinary that turnover and profits ran at an all-time high.

The way we look at our pipeline of future business totally changed as a result. We acknowledge that we have an advantage over our business competition – but we are not ashamed to say the Lord is the best Managing Director, Director of Marketing, Director of Finance and Operations we could possibly have.

Call to Galilee

In the John 21 scenario, it is safe to assume that the disciples had to land the heavy nets and doubtless clean the fish and get them ready for market. And so we embarked on an incredibly busy time with everyone working at full stretch. The major contracts were not without their challenges and client difficulties, with regular calls for team prayer. And each time the Lord gave a prophetic answer, the scriptures He gave were all about Jesus in His ministry around Galilee. On a Skype call with a colleague we both wondered out loud if God was calling us to go to Galilee as a company. A bizarre notion, you might well think.

When it came to our annual retreat in autumn 2011 (we still set three days aside despite our stretching client work), I decided to take the bull by the horns on the Thursday evening and open myself up to ridicule by my colleagues by suggesting the Lord was calling us to go to Galilee.

The suggestion was met by some joyful cries of agreement, some incredulity, but also a sceptical 'why would the Lord call us to Galilee when we meet him here?' from our Finance Director. I recall going to bed that night wrestling with the thought I had just committed the classic error of trying to second-guess God with a 'good idea' in the guise of a 'God idea'.

Every morning at the retreat centre there is a short time of prayer and contemplation for fifteen minutes led by one of the Ammerdown residents. On the Friday morning the resident brother leading the time of prayer read a single verse of scripture with a deep and resounding voice. It was Matthew 28:16:

> *Then the eleven disciples went to Galilee, to the mountain where Jesus had told them to go.*

Everyone from the company was there, sitting in a circle, and we looked at each other in amazement. As we left the chapel, my Finance

Director colleague said to me, 'So have you booked the tickets?' The call had been confirmed.

The next question, of course, was 'Why?' It was not to be a commercial or marketing trip – it was simply a call to go and meet the Master in Galilee.

In a profound sense it became a major strategic review of the company, something we hadn't done since our founding eight years earlier. It was not exactly the type of strategic business investment we had expected to build into the company budget that year, but we decided to act on the word, be obedient and planned for a party of fourteen to go to Galilee and Jerusalem shortly after Passover 2013, including our colleague Tim from New Zealand.

Because the Lord had called the whole company to go, it meant we effectively had to plan to close the company down for a week – a whole week with no fee-earning work, no marketing activity, no normal meetings, at a cost to the directors of £18,000.

Everyone was given the time to go on the trip – it did not count as annual leave. Probably not the kind of business strategy investment to get *Dragon's Den* support.

It is fair to say that, given the security situation in Israel – civil war in neighbouring Syria, regular outbreaks of violence in Gaza and the West Bank, etc. – there were some significant moments of anxiety and doubt about pursuing the call over the course of the year of planning. We were, however, set on being obedient to God's call regardless of how it may have seemed in business terms.

In our business, clients normally contract us for a specific assignment over a specific time period. Just a couple of weeks before we were due to fly out, a couple of current clients said they would like to contract ahead with us and 'pre-buy' our services. This had never happened to us before. One of the clients pre-committed to the second largest contract sum in the history of the company without actually defining all the assignments. What's more, they said they wanted to pay us up front! The Lord was clearly blessing us and allowing us to go off on our company pilgrimage in the knowledge that our order books were healthy for when we returned.

We spent a most incredible week in both Galilee and Jerusalem.

On the first morning we had communion on a boat just off the shore of the Church of the Primacy, the scene of the John 21 breakfast. Our Israeli guide was curious why a commercial company should want to follow the Master's footsteps in Galilee, and we told him the story of the John 21 prophetic word that had brought us there. He instantly explained that in Hebrew every number has a corresponding meaning in letters and words, and that the number 153 (fish in the net) means 'I am God'. It was a truly holy moment of revelation and confirmation for us as a company of our call from God.

It was a profound time where the Lord spoke to us both corporately and individually, with a clear strategic mandate for the business. The whole business team were able to reconfirm profoundly our vision and refresh our strategic calling and mission together in fellowship.

The pre-ordered work before we went was more than enough for us to glorify God and thank Him for His provision. But that is not all He did.

Those of you in business know the importance of cash flow and that unpaid invoices can be the bane of your corporate life. Well, the Lord got us to close our business down for a week, which of course meant we couldn't do the usual stuff like chasing unpaid invoices or checking the cash flow and cash balances. What happened?

In the week we were away we had a flood of paid invoices. We were left with only one unpaid invoice more than a month old. We received £240,000 in paid advance invoices for work we had yet to do over the coming four to six months. We ended up with four times our normal level of cash in the bank reserve than usual.

Not only had the Lord filled our order books *before* we went away, but He filled our bank account *while* we were away!

How on earth did that happen?

Despite the total lack of 'business logic', we had been obedient to the Lord's call and the directors were unified in our commitment to go. He gave us our mandate and it was clear He was guiding our path.

Consecration on Mount Carmel

On the trip we had a time of corporate encounter with God when we had the privilege of spending an afternoon with David and Karen Davis in the worship hall at Ha Carmel on Mount Carmel. The Lord spoke to us prophetically through David that we had to consecrate ourselves to Him, and 'follow the Ark' (the Ark of the Covenant).

The week-long trip to Israel was so full of special moments that when we got back to the UK and business as usual, it won't surprise you to know there were a few loose ends we forgot to follow up. But more of that in a moment.

We got back to the UK and were overawed with how God had filled our bank account while we were away, with every unpaid invoice getting paid and our bank balance quadrupling in a week. Plus we had work for several months ahead. Gross and net profits were good.

A picture is worth a thousand words, so in the following graph you can see how our profits grew in the three months between April and June after being in Israel.

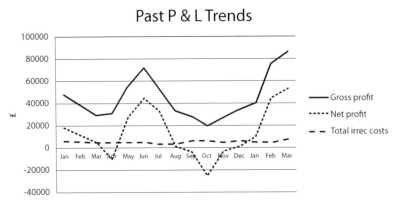

You just have to read the graph to see what happened next. From July onwards the profits began to slide and the work started to run out. We weren't getting any new orders, we made losses every month between August and December, the bank balance was gradually going down, and we came to a point in December where we were just able to pay staff salaries on time when an overdue invoice was paid a day or so before the payroll run.

What had happened?

While we were all at peace because we knew the Lord's promise to fill our nets, it is fair to say we were perplexed. Then in October, when we were praying for new orders and work for the team, He showed us that in our business coming back from Israel we forgot the command to consecrate ourselves. This time He really did have our full attention!

As a company we embarked on forty days of prayer and fasting – the fasting was left for each of us to decide before God what He would have us do, but the prayer had a disciplined schedule of daily scripture to follow for the forty days. We started in October and finished mid-December.

Now have another look at the profits graph. You guessed it. Once we obeyed the Lord to consecrate the company both corporately and personally, the orders started to come back in. A trickle of new work in late December became a flood of work and new invitations in January. In March our revenues were the second highest ever (the highest was when the Lord filled our nets for the first time in summer 2011) and we made our highest ever monthly gross profit in the nine-year history of the company.

At our team meeting in March the Lord spoke to us again. He said to remember to consecrate ourselves and the company not only in the times of lack, but in the times of abundance. A salutary reminder indeed that both busyness and complacency can be the enemies of faith.

Spirit of generosity

The Lord loves a cheerful giver (2 Corinthians 9:7) and in Luke 6:38 Jesus teaches:

How on Earth Did That Happen?

Give, and it will be given to you. A good measure, pressed down,
shaken together and running over, will be poured into your lap.

That means the principles of giving and tithing feature strongly in our policy and practice in Tricordant. We do this in four main ways.

Firstly we give away our Intellectual Property without charge or licensing. We train individual independent consultants for free if they and we feel they would benefit from knowing our consulting models and methods in a deeper way. We ask that users acknowledge the source of our consulting models, tools and methods if they wish to use them. But we believe they were freely given to us by God's grace, and are principally based on the revelation and theology of the Trinity. So it would be a bit perverse to ask people to pay to use them.

Secondly we tithe our profits. Malachi 3:6-12 speaks clearly of the critical nature of the tithe in the covenant relationship of God with His people:

'I the LORD do not change. So you, the descendants of Jacob, are not destroyed.
Ever since the time of your forefathers you have turned away from my
decrees and have not kept them. Return to me, and I will return to you,'
says the LORD Almighty. 'But you ask, "How are we to return?" Will a
man rob God? Yet you rob me. But you ask, "How do we rob you?" In
tithes and offerings. You are under a curse – the whole nation of you
– because you are robbing me. Bring the whole tithe into the storehouse,
that there may be food in my house. Test me in this,' says the LORD Almighty,
'and see if I will not throw open the floodgates of heaven and pour out so
much blessing that you will not have room enough for it. I will prevent
pests from devouring your crops, and the vines in your fields will not cast
their fruit,' says the LORD Almighty. 'Then all the nations will call you
blessed, for yours will be a delightful land,' says the LORD Almighty.

We are conscious that tithing can be a contentious issue in a company setting and can be interpreted in varying ways. I am aware of Christian companies tithing from turnover, from gross profit and from net profit. In Tricordant we come from a variety of denominations, each with their own interpretation of tithing, and we have settled on tithing the net profit of the company. We commit the net profit of the company into a charitable vehicle, the Tricordant Foundation, which we set up for the purpose of giving away from ourselves, and all members of the company have nominations rights to seek sponsorship or grant funding for charitable enterprises.

Thirdly we tithe our time. We allow everyone the ability to spend up to 10 per cent of employed time each week on pro-bono work, charitable work or 'worthy causes'. In practice it means people shift their time and effort around to get the company work done, but the policy nevertheless legitimises everyone's ability to give of their time in normal working hours to causes close to their hearts.

Fourthly we run regular development and learning events for our network of associates at minimal costs, requesting donations only to cover the cost of hiring accommodation and providing lunch. We also run Thought Network workshops for current and previous clients. These are all opportunities for colleagues and peers to gather, network and exchange ideas at very low cost.

Spiritual armour

Much of our pro-bono work comes, unsurprisingly, in work for our respective churches. Occasionally, however, we are asked to work with other Christian organisations. And it's through an illustration of the wider work that I want to communicate the need to constantly wear the full armour of God in all we do, especially when going into heavily contested spiritual places.

In 2014 we were privileged to be invited to work with the executive team of a global Christian organisation based in New York on a couple of major projects impacting the global unity and reach of the Christian faith. We agreed to do so as pro-bono consulting but with reimbursement of costs for accommodation and flights where necessary. Alastair, Simon and I were all heavily involved in the work.

As an aside I mention the reimbursement of costs as a practical point for any business invited to do pro-bono work as it signifies the recipients have some 'skin in the game' rather than receiving a pure 'freebie'. On other occasions we have specified the number of days we will give pro-bono, beyond which we would expect payment, which has led the client to use us where we can genuinely add most value and not simply because we are there and free of charge.

To return to the story, once we engaged with the client we started to experience another period of business drought. We didn't associate this with our client engagement until our website was hacked. Our website had been designed by a Christian friend and web-developer, and then handed over for routine maintenance and running to the company running our IT technical support. One morning David, the website developer, just 'happened' to open our site and spot it had not been backed up. While he was not responsible for backing up the site, he just did it spontaneously. Within five minutes the site was hacked and taken out completely, removing thousands of files and leaving behind only a package of Koranic verse that could not be traced. Evidently the Holy Spirit had prompted David ahead of the attack and our website could be quickly restored with added security. Needless to say David now has the maintenance contract too!

The week before the workshop I became aware that some deep divisions had erupted in the client's executive team and that I was likely to experience a 'lions' den'. Hard to conceive in such a Christian body, I know, but real nonetheless. So it was with added spiritual vigilance that I went to New York to deliver a two-day leadership development workshop for the executive team.

I had planned the two days quite meticulously, but also in the knowledge from previous experience that God often has other plans for our interventions. On this occasion I was woken by the Holy Spirit at 4:30 in the morning before day one of the workshop, which was due to start at 9 am. The Holy Spirit told me to ditch my plan and, instead, 'let the Word do the work'. When I asked which part of the

Word, He gave me four scriptures and also showed me how to do the work and the method to follow – and if you are a natural planner like me you will know how important that last bit was to allow me to get back to sleep!

As soon as I walked into the room where the workshop was being held I understood what was going on in the Spirit. The room was on the twenty-first floor of an office block, with panoramic views on two sides over the River Hudson and looking directly down over the site of the 9/11 World Trade Centre terrorist atrocity. If you have ever been to the Old City of Jerusalem and experienced the spiritual clash of kingdoms in a single concentrated geographic place, you will have some appreciation of the spiritual clash of kingdoms I saw in the commercial heart of New York at that moment. I also understood that we were being attacked as a business because we had engaged with a Christian organisation with missional vision for the world. And that understanding gave me the freedom I needed to let the executive team know that our business had been under attack since we engaged with them, and that was because they were under spiritual attack from an enemy determined to divide and disable them. I was then able to tell them that the programme had been changed by the Holy Spirit that morning at 4:30 am and set them to pray and seek God both individually and in paired conversations over the scriptures he had given me for them. This really was an occasion when my consulting method skills had to be absolutely sharp for the next couple of hours to be able to deliver on God's purpose for the team.

The resulting two hours in the presence of God's Word were fundamental to their survival as a team. One of them said they were so exhausted by their constant international travelling schedules that they rarely, if ever, got time to sit and meditate on the Word of God for themselves and their work. An International Council member who was present for the morning as an observer said she had learned more about them as seven people and as a team in two hours than she had in three years as a Council member.

That two-hour session was a powerful time led by the Holy Spirit and, of course, changed the whole plan for the rest of the two days. The issues of conflict dividing them as a team came into the light without being forced and a deep work of reconciliation and forgiveness was done on the second day, setting them up perfectly for their following morning together to complete their work and make their key decisions.

The consultant in me was left at the end of day two having to go and catch a plane without completing my planned agenda, and frustrated that I would not be present for their key reflections and decisions at the end of their three days together. But I was at peace knowing God was doing a sovereign work among them and they had to complete their work under His supervision rather than mine.

I was not prepared, however, for the outpouring of God's grace in the feedback I received in the following couple of days individually from each and every member of the team. I will use just one quote:

The meetings are over and I now have a few quiet moments to reflect more on what we have just been through with the xxx ExT. I began to feel an overwhelming sense of gratitude to God for having orchestrated something quite amazing. The role that you and Tricordant played in this is inestimable. So, I would like to personally tell you how grateful I am for what you did for us as a team. You were amazingly sensitive to the Holy Spirit and I think saved our organisation.

Bearing in mind the organisation was founded over 150 years earlier that last sentence brought me to tears of gratitude to God. And this was from a team member I later discovered to be really sceptical about bringing consultants in to help!

One of my reasons for telling this story is because it felt like the single most rewarding piece of consulting work I had ever done. It felt like the complete alignment between the skills and gifts God has given me with the work of the Holy Spirit, and for a cause way beyond the commercial benefit of Tricordant. It left me thinking 'How on earth did we get to do that work?' *and* 'How on earth did that happen?'

It also taught me that doing God's work in a business setting really can be about storing up treasure in heaven, not just adding to the bottom line.

Sabbath rest

Developments in technology and instant digital communications worldwide have been absolutely transformational in the way business is conducted in the twenty-first century. In my case the ability to work flexibly from home, to take the office with me on a hand-held device when I travel, to hold worldwide conferences over Skype or share live working documents with colleagues through cloud technology, have all been amazing enablers for quick and responsive consulting practice.

The technology we use today will, however, soon be obsolete as technology evolves further and faster than anyone can imagine. But it's unlikely the digital revolution will make it easier to leave our work behind.

The 'always-on' nature of digital communications is great for the performance of business and work. It's totally possible nowadays to work 24/7, dealing with Australia and New Zealand while Europe is sleeping, and vice-versa.

The fact that we can work 24/7, however, doesn't mean we should. There are clear dangers to never being away from work and never resting.

The importance of Sabbath rest was another lesson I had to learn the hard way.

Exodus 20:8-10 says:

Remember the Sabbath day by keeping it holy. Six days you shall labour and do all your work, but the seventh day is a Sabbath to the LORD your God. On it you shall not do any work.

While interpretation and application of the Sabbath differs in contemporary Christianity, the biblical principle of working six days and resting on the seventh is very clear. I have friends who have knowingly prejudiced their careers for the principle of not working on a Sunday in the retail sector and I have friends who believe it's a principle for finding a full day (24 hours) of rest without work at some time in the week. In my estimation it is not an issue of religious observance or legalism, it is a matter of the heart for each believer to work out personally with God.

Strangely enough, when I was working as a CEO in large organisations, I found it relatively easy to switch off at the weekend and not do any work. I could lock the office on a Friday evening, leave it behind and return both physically and mentally on a Monday morning. Naturally I had a mobile phone and as with all NHS Trusts we had senior managers on-call to cover any eventuality requiring a senior leadership decision in the evenings, nights or at weekends. I trusted the senior managers to take the right decisions and they knew I was available if necessary. That trust meant I hardly ever got called and they knew they could brief me first thing the following day if there had been anything happen of significance that I 'needed to know'.

Working in the consulting business from home, however, meant I was always within a few steps of the office. And even if I managed to keep my discipline and not get tempted to work, I was always 'doing' something.

It got to the point where my wife was regularly 'on my case' to take 'Sabbath rest' because I was always active with something. I had leadership responsibilities for loads of different stuff at church as well as my work. But like a stubborn husband I took it as nagging rather than spiritual truth. I was used to spinning lots of plates and getting away with it. And then I learned the hard way.

For two summer holidays in a row, in 2007 and 2008, I ended up being admitted to hospital after collapsing. These collapses had been a troubling pattern for some years and a friend had told me some time earlier I was suffering from stress and exhaustion, but I both denied and dismissed it and ploughed on with all my activities regardless.

On the second occasion, in 2008, my wife and I were on our way to Heathrow to catch a plane to see our youngest daughter Rachael, who was spending six months in Canada after being out in Pakistan with Youth for a Mission. We had returned from Israel only forty-eight hours earlier after visiting our middle daughter Sam who was working with a humanitarian aid organisation in Jerusalem, and we had flown home the day after visiting the Dead Sea at En Gedi, the lowest place on earth at over 400 metres below sea level.

I collapsed on the train and ended up in hospital. Of course the holiday trip was cancelled and I took the best part of three weeks to recover at home. Thankfully none of the medical investigations revealed any underlying or sinister disease. The best medical opinion I received, in a purely chance encounter in a lift lobby, was from a consultant anaesthetist, who was also the medical advisor to a diving club. He said they advised people always to leave a minimum of forty-eight hours between diving and flying because of the extremes in air pressure, and the possible cause of my collapse was flying less than a day after being at the Dead Sea. I know this is completely irrelevant to the story, but I include it anyway as a hot tip for anyone planning a trip to the Dead Sea!

When I got home after my episode in hospital, I was spending time in prayer and felt the Holy Spirit say, 'Read Psalm 23.' I had one of those instant irritable reactions (just being honest) and responded 'Lord, I know Psalm 23, why do You want me to read it?' And He replied, 'Read Psalm 23.' So I read Psalm 23:

The LORD is my shepherd, I shall not be in want. He makes me lie down in green pastures ...

The Lord was saying to me, 'If you won't lie down, I will make you lie down.' And instantly I knew the Lord had been warning me through my wife for some long time to observe Sabbath rest. It was for my own good.

So I had to evaluate, with the guidance of the Holy Spirit, how He wanted me to rest and what responsibilities I should lay down.

As a result of that episode I put in place a weekly discipline of rest, where I ensure at least one morning of the week (usually Saturday) is free from the tyranny of the alarm-clock and where I can spend time with the Lord without a work timetable or set of appointments constraining our time.

The result is that in subsequent years (eight and counting if you read this in 2017) I have been completely freed from the unexplained collapses. My friend and my wife had tried to get me to slow down for years and I had ignored them, but the Lord finally got through to me that my healing was in taking Sabbath rest.

Sabbath rest is a principle we operate in Tricordant not only because of my medical history but because it is something we all believe in and hold one another accountable for. Observing Sabbath rest, however we interpret its application, is a principle even for our personal development review conversations.

Another way in which we build biblical principles into the fabric of the company is through the practice of taking Sabbatical leave for two months after completion of seven years in the company. The leave is taken with full remuneration and does not count towards annual leave. It is seen as a time for personal spiritual and physical refreshing. Indeed this book is a product of my sabbatical time out.

Building the business or pursuing the mission?

You should have the pattern by now that there have been real peaks and troughs in our business, but also that some pretty profound stuff tends to happen at our retreats.

A close friend and colleague of Tricordant, Julie Beedon, came to our October 2014 retreat. Julie worked in the same field as us and had successfully run her own company for twenty years. As a result of the retreat Julie got a clear direction from God to close her own company and join us, and she became our fourth co-owner and director in January 2015.

Unsurprisingly (again!) the enemy didn't like what was happening. What followed in 2015 was a torrid time commercially, our cash flow was suffering, we weren't making any profits and our projections were not encouraging. We got to our annual retreat and it was apparent, in Simon's words, that God was shouting at us and we didn't seem to be listening. The company was now ten years old, the retreat was designed to be a celebration and time of thanksgiving, and there we were, feeling for the first time under genuine existential threat. So we had to listen carefully.

And as we listened we understood how we had started to stray into 'building the business' rather than pursuing the mandate and mission of the company. We had started to treat the retreat time as a 'strategy session' more than a time with God. We had started to build a staffing structure with grades and hierarchy, moving away from the founding vision of a fellowship of equals. And we had to repent and re-focus on the Lord's purposes for us and ask ourselves uncomfortable questions about how we had got to where we were, and how we could recover. We left Ammerdown knowing there was still much work to be done in prayer, especially re-aligning ourselves as directors and stewards of the company.

We re-focused the work on the mission, we made some key decisions to re-calibrate our reward system, but most of all we clung to the promises of God and stuck together in unity of spirit despite the fact we had hardly seen any dividend or bonus payments for months. The rubber had well and truly hit the road again on money, but we stayed united in spirit and purpose.

And it will come as little surprise to you, given the pattern of previous stories, to know this one turned around as well. Shortly into 2016 the contracts began to flow again and, most significantly, we were appointed by four major clients to be their Organisation Development Partners over twelve- to eighteen-month commitments.

As I write, that is where we stand. It's an on-going work, and as we aspire to be a Kingdom business we won't be surprised to encounter spiritual opposition. But the key is precisely in recognising the opposition is spiritual and God, as always, will honour our hearts as we seek to serve Him and His mission for us.

So what?

Being in business can be a real roller-coaster ride. It can be enthralling, exciting and downright scary all at the same time. That's true for all business, not just for Christians in business. In the same way as we are called to work out daily our salvation, we are called daily to live our business and work lives in faith.

I trust that business owners in particular will have found valuable pointers in this chapter. Here is a summary of the key points to consider:

- Unity of purpose and heart in the business, and most particularly among the business owners, is key to the success of the business and it sets the spiritual atmosphere.

- Unity will be tested particularly in relation to financial matters. We need to ensure our decision-making is informed by rather than driven by the financial consequences of decisions.

- We should always be praying and seeking God to guide our businesses, in the good times as well as the challenging times, and not just when there are issues to resolve.

- We should be seeking God's prophetic word for all situations, but we also need to 'test the spirits' and watch for what one of our Advisory Council wisely calls 'the serpent's tail', which looks really attractive but carries deadly poison – and do so without quenching the Holy Spirit.

- We should act on the prophetic when we know it is from God

– His solutions to business problems are often counter-intuitive and would never be taught on an MBA course!

- We should actively consecrate our companies by setting them apart for the purposes of God – easier where owners are all Christians, but a good principle nonetheless for Christian business ownership.

- Consecration means checking the way we do business has complete integrity and that we would never knowingly misrepresent, mislead or transgress the law in any way. It also means dealing honestly with all clients, staff and associates.

- Sabbath rest is a principle for all people working in our companies. We need to check it's happening not just in our own lives, but in those of our co-workers.

- Be generous. Corporate tithing is a contentious issue, and whether you believe it is scriptural or not, give anyway because God loves a cheerful giver.

- You can give of your time, your Intellectual Property, or your money. It's all giving in the Kingdom economy.

Nine

IGNITE!

∽∞∾

In 1989, when I first knew that God's hand was on my work life, that He would 'judge me according to my righteousness and my integrity', there were no resources for Christians in the workplace to guide my thinking. There were no books, no DVDs, no tapes, no preaching at church on the subject, no para-church ministries. Or so I thought. My church leaders and friends supported me, but the truth is they could only imagine how my situation felt as no-one had the business or managerial experience to guide me from a faith perspective.

Looking back it is apparent now that the Lord was starting a new move of faith in the workplace, not just in the UK but internationally. To name just two influential para-church organisations, the London Institute for Contemporary Christianity was founded by John Stott in 1982 and the International Christian Chamber of Commerce was founded by the Swedish businessman J. Gunnar Olson in 1985. Remember, however, that personal computing and the World Wide Web were only a twinkle in tech-geek eyes back then, so I had no knowledge of their resources or their mission, and no idea that my experience and conviction were shared by other believers in the market-place. And if I am brutally honest with myself, I didn't go looking much either.

Being a believer in the workplace felt like a really lonely business. I discovered a small prayer group at the hospital where I worked in 1989, but I only attended a couple of times as I felt unwelcome as a General Manager. Maybe it was me, but I experienced the group as critical of management and when I pointed out the scriptures about authority being instituted by God, even if it wasn't exercised in a godly way, and that we should be praying for the leaders, I was given short shrift. The small cell group in my church was the only place people took an active interest in each other's work lives.

I thank God for the radical change over the last twenty years, and that there are now so many resources and tools for Christians at work, whatever their field or profession. There are numerous conferences and para-church organisations where Christians can be fed and equipped.

One thing that has not changed, however, is the continuing sense of isolation for most Christians in their everyday workplaces. I am convinced this spirit of isolation is one of the enemy's principal tools for suppressing God's Spirit in our workplaces and businesses. It is one thing being able to access inspirational resources from excellent ministries, but something completely different being the 'church at work' and part of a fellowship of believers to pray about your work challenges and stand with you in faith to see God's Spirit rule and reign in your workplace and business. I think the big challenge is for the local church to be activated and pursuing the mission in the marketplace through the people who are anointed to be there and gifted by God for that environment.

Church leaders who 'get' the centrality of business and the workplace to contemporary Christian life are thankfully growing in number (and I count my own senior pastor among them) but are still a rare breed. My experience in the 1990s was that my church leaders knew about and respected my work and the ways in which God was blessing what I did through His miracles. Most of their working life experience, however, had been in full-time church ministry, so what I was describing was an alien world to them and I suspect they saw it as 'Roger's thing' rather than a move of God to transform society.

The change for me came in around 2005 when a small group of us in business got together and, with the full backing of our senior pastor Clive Urquhart, ran a series of workshops and seminars for the church on workplace-related subjects that were all about integrating faith, enterprise and work. While the workshop programme lasted about six months and the early wave of enthusiasm abated, out of them we launched a monthly Saturday breakfast called Ignite as an opportunity to pray with and encourage one another. And as with the experience of the workshops, the administrative burden soon grew and the numbers attending diminished.

For a variety of good and legitimate reasons, the four of us who launched the initial programme soon became two of us. It would have been easy to fold at that point in the face of discouragement, but my friend Chris and I covenanted with one another that even if there were only the two of us we would still meet, breakfast and pray together for the business and work agenda the Lord had put on our hearts. And our covenant was genuinely tested as, for two months in a row, our breakfast prayer meeting was Chris and me plus one other. And then it started to grow again as we watered the seed with prayer and perseverance.

The key to growth was in the covenant we made, and in that God saw our faith and perseverance. I tell this story because it's all too easy to kick something off, ride the early wave of enthusiasm, and then see it wilt and die through discouragement. We console ourselves (and successfully fool ourselves sometimes) that it was clearly only 'for a season' and move on to the next good idea. Only in this case we knew in our hearts it was the right thing to do, to break down the isolation of believers in the marketplace and provide a setting for believers to integrate fully their work lives and their spiritual lives. I am convinced believers need a place to be released from the falsehood that their work lives are 'secular' and of secondary importance in the heavenly realms, and our monthly breakfasts provided that opportunity.

I offer our Ignite story as a practical way of bringing men and women of faith together to encourage one another and to pray for each other with genuine understanding of the challenges of business and workplace issues.

For what it's worth I hold dear half a dozen simple rules for how we operate Ignite:

- It is a fellowship of believers, not an organisation or a ministry.
- It is relational and not hierarchical.
- We don't 'do' marketing – the fellowship is not a marketing network opportunity.
- We create the conditions when we meet for everyone's voice to be heard and valued.
- We make it as easy as possible for people to engage through different channels to allow for differing business and family commitments.
- It is multi-denominational, valuing all expressions of faith in the Lord Jesus Christ.

In practice that means we run monthly breakfasts at a local hotel and monthly prayer meetings hosted by members of the group in their business premises, one for evenings and one elsewhere for the morning early-birds.

We also run a couple of WhatsApp groups as social media platforms to pray for each other around live business issues going on in between the meetings (the Ignite Fellowship), and also to share resources, opinions and reflections on what is happening more widely affecting the world of work and business (the Ignite Forum).

In addition we run free seminars/workshops called the Avodah Series, for the group and the 'curious' every couple of months.

At the Ignite breakfasts we encourage each other with the miracles God has worked, and we pray for each other's business issues, the bids for work, the difficult clients, the cash flow issues and all the practical things that can make or break a business. We meet in the public area of a well-known chain restaurant who are thankfully geared up for indeterminate numbers of people taking breakfast, which mercifully avoids the drudge of needing confirmed numbers for breakfast. We don't do set piece preaches or worship, and we don't have guest speakers, but we gather for fellowship, relationship, encouragement and prayer. While the public area of a chain restaurant means there are limitations on things like worship and preaching, it also means we avoid the overt expressions of differing 'churchmanship' that so often separate believers unnecessarily through style and theological differences. In other words, it doesn't 'feel' like a church meeting, but it feels like a gathering of people who love Jesus and place our faith in Him for success in our work and businesses.

The set-up is important to enable some intimacy and conversation over breakfast in small groups, and we follow that by some plenary time to share stories to glorify God and pray together. It's really important that everyone, extravert and introvert alike, has the chance for their voice to be heard. For me it's more about coordinating and hosting than leading, to establish the conditions for relationship to grow between the people. And it's great to hear how people then meet and relate to one another in their daily lives outside of the group, not just as simple business contacts but as friends.

Ignite is a safe place where people can share and receive prayer and encouragement. It never fails to be uplifting. When you throw food and fellowship together you usually get a recipe for success. So colonising a corner of a Beefeater for breakfast is an inspiration. You can tell it works, because people seldom want to leave long after the last Full English has been cleared away. What I have valued so much about Ignite is the opportunity to spend time listening to one another and the Lord, and the freedom to speak and receive words of encouragement. And even better is that week after week we see answers to those prayers as contracts are renewed, businesses unblocked and strategies formed. But I suppose above all, the strength of being together in Ignite is in knowing that we are valued in the workplace and that the world of commerce – our world – really doesn't play second-fiddle to full-time ministry when it comes to advancing the kingdom. So go on – start an Ignite in your own town!

Andrew Boyd, Freelance Journalist

But we also know in Ignite that we are fighting over contested ground. Workplaces and business can be incredibly difficult and unforgiving places for anyone, let alone Christians, if the profit motive is driving the organisation. The sphere of business, in its role at the heart of our society, is so much on God's heart that the enemy is defending it with increasing violence and deception. But as believers we carry the incredible advantage of our faith and authority in the power of the Holy Spirit, if only our hearts are right towards our work.

In *The Seven Mountain Prophecy*, Johnny Enlow writes of the economy as one of the seven major spheres of influence the Lord wants to take back from the enemy for His kingdom. Jonny identifies the principality ruling the mountain of the economy as mammon, or greed. That means it will be a battle to take it back, as the enemy is not going to give up the territory easily. We need to be aware of the powers and principalities at work, some of which are so hidden in plain sight that we just ignore them and pass them off as harmless or insignificant.

Take the City of London as an example. It is at the very heart of commerce in the UK, the square mile where the Bank of England, the London Stock Market and so many of the commercial powerhouses of the UK economy reside. The Guildhall in the City of London in turn describes itself as the City powerhouse since the twelfth century. It was established in an era when the Lord Mayor of London rivalled the monarch for influence and prestige, and where the mayor and the ruling merchant class held court, fine-tuned the laws and trading regulations that helped create London's wealth.

The Guildhall, 800 years on, is still home of the City of London Corporation, and acts as a grand setting for glittering banquets in honour of visiting Heads of State and other dignitaries, royal occasions, and receptions for major historical anniversaries. It is a rare and magnificent Grade I listed landmark. And it is overseen by two statues of mythical giants on the balcony called Gog and Magog, and variously described as the Guardians or Protectors of the City. They have been there since the sixteenth century and the reign of Henry V, and have been renewed and replaced several times over the centuries. They are jarringly out of place visually, but even more out of place spiritually in the physical centre of the UK economy.

In Revelation 19:11 to 21:8 the scripture tells how Satan is to be imprisoned for a thousand years, and how, on his release, he will rally 'the nations in the four corners of the earth, Gog and Magog,' to a final battle with Christ and His saints:

When the thousand years are over, Satan will be released from his prison and will go out to deceive the nations in the four corners of the earth – Gog and Magog – to gather them for battle. In number they are like the sand on the seashore.

Revelation 20:7-10

And yet they are viewed as harmless. Every year their seven-foot-high wicker effigies lead the procession in the annual Lord Mayor's Show. Hidden in plain sight, these two mythological demons 'protect' the physical space where the UK economy is centred. We have to wake up as believers to these spiritual realities and exercise the authority we have been given in Christ to contest this ground.

As long as our eyes are on serving God and seeking first His kingdom, and not on money as the object of our business purposes, we believers in business are no longer just a nuisance but an increasing threat to the enemy's rule of the economy. So we need to get serious – we are in a spiritual war and we have to step up in prayer. And we need to do that as a body of believers, as twos and threes who gather in the presence of the Lord to see His kingdom come on earth as it is in heaven.

> *Ignite provides me with a network of like-minded people who share a passion for keeping Christ at the centre of the sphere in which they work. It is stimulating to engage with others across a diverse range of professions who understand and 'get' the way I think and some of the challenges I face. Real people living through real issues in the workplace – looking for real answers that are Spirit-led.*
> **Sarah Holloway, Media Teacher and Film Producer**

The Ignite breakfasts and prayer meetings are all about encouraging one another and building relationship – and joining together in the spiritual battle. It's time to put on the full armour of God for the battle for the marketplace!

Through a friend who edits and produces the Christian bi-monthly newspaper *Heart of Sussex*, I have been able to publish some of the stories I have told here and also those I have been hearing and gathering, providing inspiration and a simple point of contact for believers struggling with their work and business lives. As a result, the numbers coming to the Ignite breakfast have grown, with believers from a wide variety of denominations and professions pitching up, and growing in true fellowship and unity of faith.

I was becoming aware from my friendship and church network of some amazing things God was doing in the working lives of 'ordinary' Christians, but whose stories never got known or profiled at church in the same way as healings or salvations. And yet they were just as much God's sovereign work through His faithful disciples. Here are some examples:

Do you remember Richard from chapter one, the steel fabricator/ sculptor who gets his designs in dreams and visions from the Holy

Spirit while he sleeps? I shared Richard's story through the *Heart of Sussex* and we were soon joined in the Ignite group by Stef, who had been inspired by Richard's story. She had experienced the real highs and lows of business, and was in a really difficult place, facing bankruptcy after being pushed out from the very business she had grown through entrepreneurship.

She can now tell the story of how, at her lowest ebb, with no work, no income and in danger of losing her flat, she was at the verge of breakdown. She had cried out to God for help but nothing was happening for her. Then one morning the Holy Spirit whispered to her, 'Come and have a coffee with Me.' Her reaction was similar to reactions you've heard from me earlier – she had a couple of pounds in cash and no more money and her initial response was less than graceful! But the Spirit just said, 'Won't you come and have a coffee with Me?' So she went to her favourite coffee shop, sat down, ordered the coffee she could afford, and within thirty seconds her phone rang. It was an organisation where she had applied for a job several months earlier, and now they were asking if she was still available. She kept her composure and professional voice on, but you can only imagine her rejoicing inside. She confirmed her availability, went to see them, got the job and started straight away. Within two months she was organising an exhibition in the Middle East, hosted by a crown prince, with a former UK prime minister as the guest of honour.

Another story we have shared through the *Heart of Sussex* is that of Tony and his amazing journey through profound dyslexia, from Formula 1 motorsport engineer to psychotherapist. After working for twenty-five years in engineering, eight of those years in Formula 1 motorsport, he was called to Kingdom Faith Bible College. He and his wife Rachel moved to West Sussex and he had a prophecy, from a pastor, saying that he would know the inner workings of a man's mind. Whilst at Bible College he worked as a support worker with people with learning difficulties, and really needed God's grace to work with people who were very difficult and physically violent at times. It was there that someone told him he was like a counsellor. At the time he took very little notice of the statement, but something resonated inside him. He then returned to F1 engineering and as way of stretching himself signed up for a six-week counselling skills course. It was there he found what God meant when He spoke through the pastor at Bible College and what it meant to know the inner workings of a man. He found himself reading all manner of textbooks and carrying on his studies at college, and got on to an access course for the foundation degree.

Tony had been diagnosed as profoundly dyslexic as a child and destined for special school but fortunately ended up in mainstream education. So he had always struggled with getting the written word down on paper and left school not knowing how to punctuate or spell. He wrestled with the course essays and on one occasion, after having a dyslexia test for the college, God again spoke to him as he drove home. He heard the Lord say, 'Whose report will you believe, Mine or theirs?' He knew the Lord was telling him that His report was a lot better than the one he had just got which confirmed that he was profoundly dyslexic.

When he started seeing clients he knew that counselling/psychotherapy was his call. Throughout this time he would often see a pastor friend in the church and one day, whilst they were praying, the Lord said to him, 'My grace is sufficient for you, in your weakness I am made strong.' That became the overarching scripture which got him through his foundation degree and then his honours degree.

Tony now has a successful counselling and psychotherapy practice. He struggled initially but is another one whose business fortunes turned around when he committed to tithe.

The Word of God says that He will use the foolish things of this world to confound the wise, and Tony sees himself as an absolute outworking of this truth.

The key point I want to make in this chapter is that believers need genuine fellowship with one another in common cause to be the true church of Jesus Christ in the marketplace. That way we know we aren't alone, we go together to be salt and light in the world.

So what?

To become the church of integrated spiritual, family and working lives, where Christians are released in their true vocations and callings, we have to pray and work together to break the bondages of isolation and intimidation of Christians in business and the workplace. We need to create opportunities to develop relationships with one another.

To do that we have to put practical arrangements in place to meet with and encourage one another so we can be salt and light in the businesses and workplaces through our behaviour, faith and love.

Practical steps can include:

- Finding like-minded Christians in your church or friendship groups to meet and pray with regularly about your work and business. It's not complicated, but it does have to be disciplined.

- Let your pastors know what is going on for you at work, and not just in the challenging times but as a matter of routine. Meet up for breakfast if you can before you go to work. I valued that immensely in my pastor when he put aside that time for fellowship and prayer with me.

- Invite your pastor to spend some time with you at work, even if it's just to come and have lunch with you. You would be surprised the impact it can have on your colleagues when a pastor turns up simply because they are interested in you and your work.

- Pastors – offer to visit your church members in their workplaces for lunch and to pray together, to get to understand the daily challenges they face, so you can pray for them with understanding.

- Gather a fellowship of believers to breakfast together once a month – keep a light touch on the administrative side, so it doesn't become a burden, if at all possible. Create the conditions where people can develop relationship with one another and become more than just a business opportunity.

- When you gather, give people space to glorify God and bring their requests for prayer.

- Pastors – invite speakers to your church who can ignite the spark of faith for the workplace and business.

- Set up social media groups to pray for and encourage one another on a daily basis.

- Whatever you do, just make sure you break the bondage of isolation!

Ten

NOW WHAT?

∽o∾

T hanks for sticking with me so far. I'll make this next part brief. The world of work, business and the economy is central to God's design for His creation and the welfare of His people. I'm not talking here of man-made economic models, or writing in praise of Western capitalism. I'm saying that God created mankind to work and be fruitful.

The context in which I work happens to be a market economy model. Whatever the prevailing economic model, however, believers are called to serve the Lord and to be salt and light in our communities. We are called to *avodah* – work that is service to our Lord.

For God's will to be done on earth as it is in heaven, He needs an army of business leaders, faith-filled workers, and faithful intercessors who will not only worship and serve Him through their work, but will fight the spiritual battle in heavenly places and take authority over all the power of the enemy in the marketplace.

My journey over the last twenty-five years in my work has taught me above all to place my faith in the truth of the Word of God and not to fear the circumstances I face, or the ridicule I might encounter from not-yet-believers for taking the positions I take. I know that my Father in heaven cares about my work life and the opportunity it gives me to be salt and light in the world. He made me to work and be fruitful. He made me to worship and serve Him through my work.

My story is living proof of God's faithfulness and the anointing He confers when His people commit their careers and work to Him. It is proof that when God anoints His people to lead organisations, He will do extraordinary things in those organisations to prosper them and make them outstanding, so He can be glorified.

Why has God chosen to work this way in my life? I believe one part of it is so I can tell this story to encourage His church, His people, to understand their God-given place in a world where there is no division between the sacred and the secular. It is all one. And it is to demonstrate that when our work is done in His service, He makes it prosper.

I believe God is calling His people to action and to be His church in positions of authority, to prepare the way for His kingdom, a people who will treat their work as service to the Lord, their *avodah* work to glorify God. People who live the truth of the gospel message and its relevance for now in their workplaces and their businesses. I believe He wants people to take both spiritual *and* positional authority in the major spheres of influence in society.

Our answer to His call is to re-integrate the spiritual and the so-called secular dimensions of our lives so we can answer Jesus' prayer – on earth as it is in heaven!

It's time to start believing your faith is a matter for every day of the week and not just for Sundays.

Like all things it starts with a choice, the choice to believe that my work can also be my service to God. The choice to believe that I can fulfil my call to be salt and light in the world of work where I spend so much of my waking life and where He has gifted me to be at my best.

If you want to make the choice to worship God through your work, there's no better time or place to start than now. How about starting with this simple prayer?

Lord God, I submit my work life to You. I am Your workmanship and You created me to work. You knitted me together in my mother's womb and gave me talents and gifts to be fruitful in my work. I submit all my abilities and skills to the leading of Your Holy Spirit.

My faith and trust in You are my supreme qualifications for fruitfulness in my working life. I pray that my decisions and choices will honour You and will be faithful to the truth of Your Word.

I thank You for the wisdom of Your Word to guide my path, and for the gift of Your Spirit to lead me in the ways I respond to the challenges of each working day, to lead me in the words I speak and the actions I take.

I pray You give me the courage I need to stand for righteousness in all my work and business dealings.

I consecrate my work to You as a sacrifice of praise from this day on. And I thank You that You anoint me for the task You have set for me.

Your kingdom come, Your will be done, in my work as it is in heaven.

Amen.

The simple imperative of getting this book written means I have to draw a line somewhere in my story. But I know my journey won't stop here. How about yours?

ABOUT THE AUTHOR

Roger Greene first discovered the power of God's Word in 1989 at a point of crisis in his work. This book is his testimony of how he has integrated his faith with his career, to the point where God has moved in amazing signs and wonders in his work and business life.

Roger writes from the unique perspective of a career in top leadership positions in the public, commercial and voluntary sectors in the UK over 30 years. He was a Chief Executive in the NHS for 12 years, and is now a Director of the consulting business Tricordant Ltd. He leads the Ignite fellowship of Christians from a variety of denominations in the workplace and business in the south-east of England

He believes passionately that the sacred-secular divide is a man-made falsehood that God is dismantling, and that Christians in the work-place and business have a first class spiritual calling to be His Church in the world, to usher in the Kingdom of God "on earth as it is in heaven".

Roger is married with 3 daughters and 3 grandchildren (to date!). He lives in West Sussex but says that while you can take the boy out of Liverpool, but you can never take Liverpool out of the boy!

You can find out more about the Ignite fellowship of Christians at www.ignitework.net.

How on Earth Did That Happen?

PRAYER

⌒o⌒

We hope you enjoyed this book and that it has been both a blessing and a challenge to your life and walk with God. Maybe you just got hold of it and are glancing through before starting. We made the decision as a publishing company right from the start never to take for granted that everyone has prayed a prayer to receive Jesus as their Lord, so we are including that as the finale to this book. If you have never asked Jesus into your life and would like to do that now, it's so easy. Just pray this simple prayer:

Dear Lord Jesus,
Thank You for dying on the cross for me. I believe that You gave Your life so that I could have life. When You died on the cross, You died as an innocent man who had done nothing wrong. You were paying for my sins and the debt I could never pay. I believe in You, Jesus, and receive the brand new life and fresh start that the Bible promises that I can have. Thank You for my sins forgiven, for the righteousness that comes to me as a gift from You, for hope and love beyond what I have known and the assurance of eternal life that is now mine.
Amen.

Good next moves are to get yourself a Bible that is easy to understand and begin to read. Maybe start in John so you can discover all about Jesus for yourself. Start to pray – prayer is simply talking to God – and, finally, find a church that's alive and get your life planted in it. These simple ingredients will cause your relationship with God to grow.

Why not email us and let us know if you did that so we can rejoice with you?

info@greatbiglifepublishing.com

FURTHER INFORMATION

For further information about the author of this book, or to order more copies, please contact:

Great Big Life Publishing
Empower Centre
83-87 Kingston Road
Portsmouth
Hampshire
PO2 7DX
United Kingdom
info@greatbiglifepublishing.com

ARE YOU AN AUTHOR?

∾ॐ∽

Do you have a word from God on your heart that you're looking to get published to a wider audience?

We're looking for manuscripts that identify with our own vision of bringing life-giving and relevant messages to Body of Christ. Send yours for review towards possible publication to:

Great Big Life Publishing
Empower Centre
83-87 Kingston Road
Portsmouth
Hampshire
PO2 7DX
United Kingdom
info@greatbiglifepublishing.com